Fruit
Desserts

SARAH BROWN

A committed vegetarian, yet refreshingly undoctrinaire in her approach, Sarah Brown believes in eating good healthy food and in eating well. She gives regular demonstrations and lectures, and, as national coordinator of cookery for the Vegetarian Society of the United Kingdom, runs a series of cookery courses. Well known for her highly successful BBC television series "Vegetarian Kitchen" and for her bestselling "Sarah Brown's Vegetarian Cookbook" and "Sarah Brown's Healthy Living Cookbook", she has played a major role in promoting public awareness of the link between health and diet and the widespread move towards a healthier style of eating.

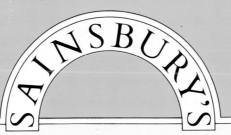

SAINSBURY'S

HEALTHY·EATING
·COOKBOOKS·

Fruit
Desserts

SARAH BROWN

CONTENTS

Fruit Desserts was conceived, edited and designed by Dorling Kindersley Limited, 9 Henrietta Street, London WC2E 8PS

Published exclusively for J Sainsbury plc, Stamford House, Stamford Street, London SE1 9LL
by Dorling Kindersley Limited, 9 Henrietta Street, London WC2 8PS

First published 1986

Copyright © 1986 by Dorling Kindersley Limited, London   Text copyright © 1986 by Sarah Elizabeth Brown Limited

ISBN 0-86318-148-1

Printed in Italy

INTRODUCTION

"An apple a day keeps the doctor away". This old maxim reminds us that fruit epitomizes healthy eating and is an important element in our diet. At the same time it is one of the most versatile, refreshing and tempting foods in existence.

WHY FRUIT IS GOOD FOR YOU

Fruit is the ideal ingredient for desserts. It contains a natural sweetener that satisfies a sweet tooth, in many cases needs no added sugar and as you develop a taste for fresh fruit, sugary puddings and cakes will begin to taste oversweet. Since most fruits contain a lot of water, they make a refreshing end to a meal and do not add many calories. They are also high in fibre (especially berries and dried fruit) which takes the form of cellulose, an aid to digestion. Most fruits are high in vitamins and minerals. They provide the best source of Vitamin C in the diet. This vitamin is needed for the maintenance of healthy connective tissue. It is also destroyed by long storage, so it is best to eat fruit as fresh as possible. Citrus fruit and berries are an especially good source of Vitamin C. Some yellow fruits, for example apricots and melons, contain carotene which is converted into Vitamin A in the body and a number of fruits are rich in potassium, magnesium and calcium.

Dried fruits are a particularly valuable addition to a healthy diet, since they offer nutrients and sweetness in a concentrated form. They make wonderful natural sweeteners in puddings and cakes and are a healthy alternative to confectionery and sugar-based snacks.

GETTING THE BEST OUT OF FRUIT

The variety of fruit – local, Continental and tropical – now available at all times of year, is enormous. The standard selection of apples, pears, oranges and bananas is now augmented by a wide range of berries and exotic tropical fruit. It is best to keep fruit in a cool place or the fridge, with the exception of bananas, papayas and mangoes which may need to go on ripening. Choose orchard fruit with unblemished skins and firm berries. Tropical fruit usually have a sweet smell when ripe and should feel firm, not hard.

Fruit desserts can be visually stunning, even fruit salads, which are so easy to prepare. For simple puddings, fruit purées, mousses and creams need very little preparation and can be sweetened by combining dried fruits with fresh varieties. For more traditional puddings, combinations of cooked fruit make delicious fillings for pies, crêpes and layered baked dishes.

WHAT IS A HEALTHY DIET?

There now seems little question that good health is dependent on a healthy diet, no smoking and plenty of exercise. But what is a healthy diet? There seem to be a bewildering number of conflicting answers against a background of tempting new products, all advertised as "natural", "healthy" and "wholesome". What are the real facts?

FOOD FASHIONS

With the development of nutritional science over the last 100 years, the major nutrients – protein, fat, carbohydrate, vitamins and minerals – appear to have fallen in and out of favour. Shortly after the war, everyone was urged to eat more protein, but today we are told that the Western world consumes too much of this expensive energy source. Recently there has been a well-publicized debate about fats: is margarine better for you than butter? Carbohydrate, once the enemy of the slimming industry is now back in favour, as a result of the pro-fibre campaign. Yet sugar, another carbohydrate, has been blamed for tooth decay, obesity and adult-onset diabetes. Each of these fashions spawn a new "diet", which in turn encourages unbalanced eating.

GETTING THE BALANCE RIGHT

All the major nutrients have distinctive and important roles to play in our diet, and it is now clear that a healthy diet means eating not only the right quantity, but also the right type of each one (see pp.90–93).

The Western diet is very high in fat, sugar and salt, and low in fibre, fresh fruit and vegetables. The guidelines for a healthy diet, summed up by the reports prepared by the National Advisory Committee on Nutrition Education and the Committee on Medical Aspects of Food Policy are:

- Eat more unrefined carbohydrates which contain fibre (see pp.90–92).

- Eat more fresh fruit and vegetables, which contain fibre as well as vitamins and minerals.

- Eat less fat, sugar and salt (see pp. 90–92).

Adopting a healthy diet that will positively help your long- and short-term health is, therefore, only a shift of emphasis, which can quickly become a way of life.

WHAT IS WRONG WITH A HIGH-FAT DIET?

High-fat diets have been clearly linked with incidence of coronary heart disease. Moreover, a high-fat diet tends to be a low-fibre diet, which is associated with intestinal disorders, constipation, diverticulitis and cancer of the colon. One further danger – on a high-fat diet, it is easy to consume excess calories, as fat contains more than twice the number of calories, weight for weight, as carbohydrate and protein. Surplus fat is stored in the body as fatty deposits, which can lead to obesity and its attendant problems of diabetes, high blood pressure and gall bladder disease. It is important to cut down your fat intake to about 30–35 per cent of the day's calories or less. There are three types of fat, which need to be distinguished according to their origin and their interaction with cholesterol.

SATURATED FATS

Mainly found in foods from animal sources (particularly red meat fat, full-fat cheeses, butter and cream), saturated fats are high in cholesterol and if they are eaten in excess, the cholesterol can be laid down as fatty deposits in the blood vessels which can lead to heart disease and atherosclerosis.

POLYUNSATURATED FATS

These fats are mainly found in foods from vegetable sources in liquid oil form usually from plant seeds, such as sunflower and safflower. They are, however, also present in solid form in grains and nuts. Although they contribute to the overall fat intake, they can lower levels of cholesterol in the blood.

MONOUNSATURATED FATS

These fats, which are found in olive oil, have no effect on cholesterol levels, but do add to daily fat intake.

The three types of fat are present in varying proportions in high-fat foods. The fat in butter, for example, contains 63 per cent saturated fat and only 3 per cent polyunsaturated, whereas the fat in polyunsaturated margarine contains 65 per cent polyunsaturated and 12 per cent saturated fat.

WHAT IS WRONG WITH A SUGAR-RICH DIET?

Sugar, or sucrose, in the form of refined white or brown sugar is all too easy to eat, but contributes only calories to a diet. Sugar not used immediately for fuel is converted into fat, encouraging weight gain. Sugar is also a principle factor in tooth decay. Highly refined carbohydrates, particularly sugar are also absorbed easily into the bloodstream, quickly increasing blood sugar levels. If the body overreacts to this, the blood sugar levels drop dramatically, leaving the desire to eat something sweet and thus creating a vicious circle. In addition, the cells that produce insulin cannot always cope with sudden concentrations of glucose and diabetes may result. Try not only to cut down on sugar in drinks and cooking, but when cutting down, take particular care to avoid manufactured foods, both sweet and savoury, where sugar comes near the top of the list of ingredients. Always check the nutritional labelling on the container.

WHY DO WE NEED LESS SALT?

There is a clear link in certain people between salt intakes and high blood pressure – a condition that can lead to circulatory problems, such as heart disease and strokes. The sodium from salt works with potassium in regulating body fluids. Excess salt upsets this balance, which puts a strain on the kidneys. In general, we eat more salt than we need. Do be aware of the amount hidden in processed foods and try not to add more during home cooking.

WHAT IS SO GOOD ABOUT FIBRE?

High-fibre foods are more filling than other foods, take longer to chew and satisfy hunger for longer, which reduces the temptation to eat between meals. They are also less completely digested, thus helping to reduce actual calorie intake. The evidence strongly suggests that lack of dietary fibre can cause cancer of the colon in addition to simple constipation. A low-fibre diet often means a high-fat, high-sugar diet with the problems that induces, including adult-onset diabetes. Only plant foods, in the form of unrefined carbohydrates, like whole grains and fresh fruit and vegetables, contain fibre and it is critical to eat more. Simply switching to high-fibre breakfast cereals, from refined flours and pastas to wholemeal, in addition to eating plenty of fresh fruit and vegetables will dramatically increase your fibre intake.

Sarah Brown

USING WHOLEFOODS

The first step in a healthy diet is to choose fresh and wholefoods that are unrefined and as close to their natural state as possible. Simply buy plenty of fresh fruit and vegetables, and use wholemeal flour, bread, pasta and pastry and health foods and whole grains, such as beans and oatmeal. When buying convenience food, select those that contain natural ingredients and the minimum of artificial colours, flavourings and preservatives. These steps alone will ensure that your diet is high in unrefined carbohydrate, rich in vitamins and minerals and lower in fat, salt and sugar.

USING THIS BOOK

The aim of this book is to translate the simple rules for health into a practical and enjoyable form. The recipes are naturally low in fat, high in fibre and unrefined ingredients, with natural sweeteners replacing sugar. Ingredients are used in their most nutritious form.

Healthy eating is not boring, nor does it involve a sacrifice. It is simply a matter of choosing and using more nutritious foods to create delicious, yet healthy meals.

USING THE RIGHT EQUIPMENT

● A blender saves a lot of time when blending liquids or making fruit purées and frothy drinks.

● A food processor is more sophisticated. It comes with a variety of attachments for mincing, grating, shredding, dicing, mixing and puréeing. It is ideal for blending, making batters, cake mixtures, dough and pastry, and also for whisking.

● If you do not have either, you will need a sieve, a whisk, a sharp knife, a mixing bowl and a wooden spoon.

WHERE TO STORE FRUIT

● Keep the following in the fridge (5–8°C): apples, apricots, ripe avocados (unripe avocados blacken at temperatures below 7°C if kept for more than 10 days), cherries, peaches, grapes, pineapples (if ripe and cut), pears, raspberries, strawberries and melon.

● Store the following in a cool place: bananas, grapefruit, lemons, unripe pineapples, oranges, mandarins, passion fruit and mangoes.

HOW LONG TO STORE FRUIT

● Keep citrus fruit for up to 3 weeks.

● Eat tropical and soft fruit within 2–4 days of ripening.

● Keep dried fruit for up to a year in an airtight container, but it will be past its best after 6 months. (Always check the "best before" date label.) A piece of citrus peel in the container helps to keep it moist.

● Keep reconstituted, cooked dried fruit in the fridge for 3–4 days.

WHAT TO DO WITH DRIED FRUIT

● Rinse in clean water, then cover with liquid (either water, unsweetened fruit juice or cold tea) and leave to soak for 8–12 hours. You could spice the soaking water with nutmeg, cinnamon or vanilla essence for extra flavour. Alternatively, place the fruit in a pan, cover with liquid and simmer for 10–15 minutes. Then leave for 1 hour.

● To cook dried fruit once it has been reconstituted, simply stew for 30–40 minutes in the soaking liquid.

USING FLAVOURINGS

Use fresh herbs and whole spices where possible but if you only have dried herbs to hand, remember you need only half the quantity.

allspice: good for fruit and yogurt drinks, puréed fruit desserts, cakes, puddings.
angelica: used as a garnish; has a sweet, musky, aromatic fragrance.
cinnamon: warm, sweet aromatic flavour, excellent with apples and pears.
ginger: hot, pungent, spicy flavour, good in biscuits and with mild fruit.
mint: delicious in fruit salads, ice creams, mousses and sauces; has a mild, slightly sweet flavour.
rosemary: highly aromatic, tastes slightly of pine; has a strong flavour, good in fruit dishes with apple.

USING HEALTHY ALTERNATIVES

● Yogurt, smetana, silken tofu and skimmed milk soft cheeses make excellent alternatives to cream.

● Concentrated juice, honey and fruit purées make good alternatives to sugar.

● Wholemeal flour makes a healthier pastry or batter than white flour.

INGREDIENTS

Part of the joy of cooking is choosing the ingredients – especially when this involves selecting fresh fruit, herbs and vegetables and trying out new, unusual and exotic foods.

Always buy the freshest ingredients possible – they contain more vitamins and minerals and have a much better flavour and texture than preserved foods. Grains, pulses, flours, cereals and dried fruit, herbs and spices, however, generally keep for at least 3 months, so it is worth maintaining a small store of basic dry ingredients, particularly those that need to be soaked or cooked in advance. It is also useful to keep a small selection of canned or bottled fruit, vegetables and beans for emergencies. But try to select those without artificial additives or a high sugar or salt content and use them by the "best before" date.

The range of "healthy" ingredients has grown dramatically in recent years, particularly low-fat, reduced sugar, reduced salt, high fibre and vegetarian alternatives to traditional foods. These open the way to both a healthier and a more varied diet and offer endless possibilities for personal variations. The success of a recipe depends as much on the quality of the raw materials as on the way you combine them. In many cases, it is better to use a fresh alternative than to use the specified ingredient if it is not at its best – use fresh, ripe peaches, for example, in place of hard or over-ripe nectarines.

The following pages illustrate many of the familiar and the unusual ingredients found in the recipes in this book – from staples, to flavourings and dairy products. The section acts as both an identification guide and a reference source. You will find advice on choosing and storing food, together with useful information about the origins, culinary applications and nutritional value of specific ingredients. For more detailed nutritional information, see pages 90–93.

CITRUS AND TROPICAL FRUITS

An exciting variety of tropical fruits are now imported from around the world at all times of year. They are best bought slightly under-ripe and allowed to ripen at home to catch them at their best. Citrus fruit, which will keep for a long time in a cool place, are also available all the year round and are an excellent concentrated source of Vitamin C.

BANANA

Rich in Vitamins B_6 and folic acid, bananas taste best when the skins are yellow, tinged with brown. The soft flesh of brown-skinned bananas makes a good purée.

LYCHEES

The winter fruit of a slow-growing Chinese tree, lychees will keep refrigerated for 3 months. When the knobbled skins turn red, the soft, white flesh is ready to eat.

KUMQUATS

The tiniest of citrus fruits, the Chinese "golden orange" is eaten whole with its rind. It is ripe when slightly soft.

PAW-PAW (Papaya)

The rich, peach-flavoured flesh is ready to eat when the skin turns from green to yellow. The black seeds make a good garnish.

PINEAPPLE

This sweet, tropical fruit is ripe when the leaves are easily detached and the skin is golden not green.

PASSION FRUIT

When the dark skin starts to wrinkle, the fragrant, seedy pulp is ripe to eat. Choose the largest fruit available for the juiciest pulp.

KIWI FRUIT

(Chinese gooseberry)

These delicate New Zealand fruit are rich in Vitamin C. The season is May–July, but they freeze well for up to 6 months.

LEMON

High in fibre, low in calories and rich in Vitamin C and calcium, lemons are best in February and March. Choose the largest and smoothest.

LIME

Slightly sweeter and more delicate than lemons, sweet limes make a refreshing flavouring. The freshest limes have dark, shiny, tight skins.

ORANGES

There are several types of sweet orange. The main varieties are Shamouti, Valencia, navel and blood, all high in Vitamin C. Navels have a thicker skin and are easier to peel, while blood oranges have a sweeter, redder flesh than normal oranges.

PINK GRAPEFRUIT

Grapefruit are high in Vitamin C and are thought to contain an enzyme that speeds metabolism. The pink variety are often juicier than the white and are sweet enough to eat without added sugar.

BERRIES ᴬᴺᴰ STONE FRUIT

Berries and stone fruit are high in fibre, Vitamin C and in some cases, iron. To enjoy the fruit at its best, buy it in season, choose the freshest available and eat it soon after ripening. Handle soft fruit carefully to avoid bruising and refrigerate berries without washing to prevent loss of vitamins.

BLACKBERRIES

Found either cultivated or wild in the hedgerows in the autumn, blackberries are a good source of fibre. When picking your own for cooking, include some red berries for a piquant flavour.

BLACK CHERRIES

There are two species of cherry; sweet, eating cherries with either red or black (left) skins, and bitter cherries, such as Morellos, for cooking.

REDCURRANTS

Slightly sweeter than other currants, but equally rich in Vitamin C, the red variety can be eaten raw when ripe.

COOKING PLUM

Available all year round, except in early spring, plums should be cooked when ripe for the sweetest flavour.

WILD STRAWBERRIES

Usually only found in August and September, these small, iron-rich berries have a stronger, richer taste than the cultivated variety.

CULTIVATED STRAWBERRIES

Since they lose flavour and texture when frozen, it is best to buy fresh strawberries, now available at most times of year.

DESSERT PLUM

Best eaten soon after they are ripe, dessert plums, such as Victorias (above) should have a firm, unblemished skin.

GREENGAGE

This sweet variety of dessert plum that turns amber when fully ripe is in season only from September to mid-October.

BLUEBERRIES

Like most soft fruit, blueberries are available in mid-summer. They have a tart flavour and are eaten raw or cooked with natural sweetening.

BLACKCURRANTS

Rich in Vitamin C and iron, blackcurrants make an excellent dessert fruit and are always eaten cooked.

CRANBERRIES

These winter berries, which are grown in the USA, keep and freeze well inside their protective, waxy skins.

WHITECURRANTS

This albino currant is slightly sweeter than other currants and equally rich in Vitamin C.

LOGANBERRIES

This blackberry hybrid tastes more like a raspberry. It is good both raw and cooked.

RASPBERRIES

Red, white and black raspberries are all rich in iron and freeze more successfully than strawberries. Avoid punnets with stains at the base.

APRICOT

There are two crops, May–August and December–February. When eating raw, choose ripe, dark-coloured fruit for a sweet flavour. Canned apricots retain a good flavour and when dried are rich in Vitamin A and iron.

PEACH

There are two types of peach – "freestone" for eating and "clingstone" for cooking. The smaller and paler fruits often have the best flavour.

NECTARINE

A cross between a peach and a plum, the smooth-skinned nectarine should be eaten when pink and slightly soft.

VINES, MELONS ～ TOP FRUIT

Vines, ground runners and fruit trees usually yield their fruit in the late summer and autumn, although many imported varieties are available throughout the year. Tree (top) fruit are best bought slightly under-ripe, stored in a cool, dry place and eaten when ripe. Vine fruit (grapes) and fruit which grow on ground runners are easily bruised, so should be handled carefully.

WHITE GRAPES

Of the many varieties of wine and dessert grapes, the Muscat and Almeira are perhaps the best for eating. These are available at most times of year.

SEEDLESS WHITE GRAPES

Available from January to June, the seedless varieties of grape are generally smaller and sweeter than seeded.

BLACK GRAPES

The tough skin on black grapes adds colour and fibre to desserts. All grapes are rich in fructose.

CANTALOUPE MELON

The charentais, (left), is a small, sweet variety of the cantaloupe and equally high in Vitamin A and folic acid. Cut pieces will keep for up to 2 days if sealed from the air.

WATERMELON

The watermelon, a different genus from other melons, contains 91 per cent water. Serve it cold for a refreshing, low-calorie dessert.

HONEYDEW MELON

Like other melons, the honeydew is available all year round and is ripe when the stalk end gives slightly.

COX'S ORANGE PIPPIN

Crisp, juicy and highly flavoured, this excellent eating apple is found between September and May. Sturmers have a similarly good flavour.

GREEN DESSERT APPLE

The Granny Smith, originally from Australia, has a distinctively sharp, crisp flavour and a good colour. It is available year-round.

RED DESSERT APPLE

The Red Delicious from America has a sweet flavour and an attractive colour for fruit salads and other desserts. The Danish Spartan and the French Starking are also good red eating apples with a sweet flavour.

POMEGRANATE

Valued for its sweet seeds, which can be eaten raw, combined with other fruit or used to make drinks, the pomegranate is available in the late autumn.

MANGO

The red and the two green/yellow varieties are all rich in Vitamin A, and should be eaten when they feel slightly soft and smell ripe.

WILLIAM PEAR

A good late summer dessert pear, the William is best bought when firm and eaten as soon as it is ripe.

PACKHAM PEAR

Crisper and sharper than the William, the Packham is excellent raw or cooked and is in season from May to August.

NUTS AND DRIED FRUIT

Nuts are a good source of protein, vitamins and minerals, while dried fruit contain concentrated amounts of iron and other minerals, B and C Vitamins and sugar. Dried fruit will keep for over 6 months in an airtight container. Shelled nuts should be stored in a cool, dry place and used as soon as possible. Unshelled and unsalted nuts keep longer.

ALMONDS

From a Mediterranean tree related to the peach, almonds are rich in protein, Vitamin B_2, folic acid and minerals. Sweet almonds are available whole, roasted, salted and sugared.

WALNUTS

Walnuts and pecans are rich in protein, unsaturated fat, minerals and vitamins, particularly B_6, and are sold unsalted.

HAZELNUTS

Also known as filberts and cobs, hazelnuts contain less fat than other nuts but are rich in the B Vitamins, folic acid and zinc.

SESAME SEEDS

This oil-rich Indian seed makes a nutritious snack or garnish and when ground into a paste, is called "tahini".

CASHEW NUTS

Although high in calories and fat, cashews are full of valuable vitamins and minerals. The healthiest type are roasted and unsalted.

SULTANAS

These dried grapes are larger and sweeter than raisins and equally high in Vitamin B_6 and potassium.

PINE KERNELS

The seeds of the Mediterranean stone pine, known as pignoli, are sold shelled, roasted and sometimes salted.

DRIED PEACHES

An excellent source of
iron, dried peaches can be
easily reconstituted by
soaking in fresh water.

DRIED BANANA

Fresh bananas are peeled, sliced
lengthways and dried to make a
sweet, nutritious ingredient or
snack. Banana chips, which are
deep-fried, are less healthy.

DESICCATED COCONUT

Dried, grated coconut, which makes an
excellent flavouring, is also sold as
flakes, powder or compressed into
blocks known as creamed coconut.

DRIED APRICOTS

Dried apricots are extremely
high in protein, fibre, and
Vitamins A and C. Try to
avoid those preserved in sugar.

DRIED DATES

High in Vitamin A and
niacin, dried dessert
dates are sold unstoned,
while cooking dates are
sold stoned in blocks.

PRUNES

These dried black plums are low in
calories, but high in potassium and
fibre and the tenderized variety can be
cooked in 8 minutes. Prunes are sold
with or without stones.

DRIED FIGS

Iron-rich and high in fibre, dried figs
are also high in sugar, so avoid those
with an added dusting of sugar.

HUNZA APRICOTS

Sun-dried naturally, and
preserved without the aid of
sulphur, these Himalayan fruit
have a wonderful flavour and
are rich in protein, fibre, iron
and Vitamins A and C.

DAIRY PRODUCE ∽ ALTERNATIVES

The wide range of low-fat dairy products now on the market are rich in protein, calcium and Vitamins A, B_{12} (essential in a vegetarian diet) and D, and help to reduce saturated fat intakes. Vegetarian, rennet-free cheeses and soya-based milk products are also now widely available. Store in the fridge.

FIRM TOFU

Low in fat and high in protein, firm tofu is made from the heavily pressed curds of the soya bean. Soft tofu is lightly pressed.

SKIMMED MILK

With the cream skimmed off, this milk contains only 0.1 per cent fat, while it retains all the water-soluble vitamins and minerals of whole milk.

SMETANA

An excellent, low-fat substitute for cream, smetana is a soured mixture of single cream and skimmed milk and contains 5–10 per cent fat.

SILKEN TOFU

Silken tofu is a mixture of soya curds and whey and has a smooth texture, ideal for creamy, low-fat desserts.

YOGURT

Whole or skimmed milk injected with bacteria and left to ferment produces yogurt. Unflavoured "natural" yogurt made from skimmed milk contains the least fat.

SKIMMED MILK SOFT CHEESE

(quark)

Made from semi-skimmed or skimmed milk, quark is a smooth, salt-free cheese with a slightly sharp taste.

COTTAGE CHEESE

Made from cooked, skimmed cow's milk, this unripened cheese is a low-fat version of curd cheese.

CURD CHEESE

Made from the separated curds of whole cow's milk and set without rennet, curd cheese contains 11 per cent fat and has a slightly acid flavour.

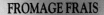

FROMAGE FRAIS

This non-fermented, non-cured, unsalted cheese is made from cooked goat's or cow's milk and cream. Varieties with a very low fat content are available.

RICOTTA

This very low-fat, unripened Italian soft cheese is made from the whey, not the curds of cow's or goat's milk. It can be bought by weight, as a whole cake, or in hardened form for grating.

FLAVOURINGS AND SPICES

There is now a wide range of healthy alternatives to traditional flavourings, particularly natural sweeteners. Spices, which also add flavour to desserts, are best used fresh and if ground, should be stored in an airtight container.

CONCENTRATED APPLE JUICE

An excellent natural sweetener in fruit desserts and sauces, "CA is rich in Vitamin C and will keep in the fridge for 3 weeks.

MALT EXTRACT

Otherwise known as barley syrup, malt is not as sweet as normal syrup and contains iron and B Vitamins.

HONEY

Mineral-rich, pure honey is much sweeter than sugar, so you need smaller quantities.

CLOVES

The strong-tasting buds of a species of myrtle tree, cloves are usually used whole, but the heads can be ground for a more diluted spice.

AGAR-AGAR FLAKES

This vegetarian setting agent is sold as powder or flakes.

PEAR AND APPLE SPREAD

This fruit purée, a Vitamin C-rich spread, makes a healthy natural sweetener and thickener.

GROUND GINGER

The dried root of the ginger plant is available fresh and unpeeled or ground into a powder.

GROUND NUTMEG

This powder comes from the dried nut contained within a husk known as mace. Buy whole where possible and grate as required.

CAROB POWDER

Lower in fat but sweeter than cocoa, this caffeine-free powder is a healthy alternative to chocolate.

TAHINI

A paste made from ground sesame seeds, tahini is rich in protein and calcium.

FRESH FRUIT

Raw, fresh fruit makes a refreshing end to a filling meal. Since all these dishes are uncooked, the fruit retains all its vitamins and minerals, and if the skin is left on, adds plenty of fibre. Many of these desserts also make excellent breakfast dishes, served with yogurt or muesli.

GOLDEN FRUIT SALAD

INGREDIENTS

12oz (375g) watermelon
1 pomegranate
8oz (250g) fresh pineapple
2 nectarines

•

NUTRITION PROFILE

This fruit dessert is low in fat and calories and a good source of Vitamins A and C.

• Per portion •
Carbohydrate: 24.8g
Protein: 1.7g **Fibre:** 2.9g
Fat: 0.3g **Calories:** 110

There is sometimes no need to add extra liquid or sugar to a fruit salad, since most fruits provide plenty of natural juice. For balance, choose some watery ingredients such as melon for the liquid, and some sweet fruits such as nectarines for the flavour.

Preparation time: 20 mins (plus chilling time)
Serves 4–6

METHOD

1. Remove the peel and the seeds from the watermelon and chop the flesh into medium chunks.

2. Slice the pomegranate in half and remove all the seeds, taking care not to put any yellow pith into the salad.

3. Cut the pineapple flesh into chunks. Stone and slice the nectarines.

4. Mix all the fruit carefully together in a serving bowl and refrigerate. Serve chilled.

Illustrated on page 22

MELON ~AND~ STRAWBERRY SALAD
WITH CREAMY ORANGE TOPPING

INGREDIENTS

1lb (500g) Galia melon
8oz (250g) strawberries, hulled
7oz (200g) skimmed milk soft
cheese (quark)
juice of 1 large orange
2–3 drops vanilla essence

•

NUTRITION PROFILE

*This high-protein dessert is low in fat and
calories. It is a rich source of Vitamin C
and contains useful amounts of iron
and calcium.*

• Per portion •
Carbohydrate: 12.8g
Protein: 7.8g   **Fibre:** 2.5g
Fat: 0.2g   **Calories:** 80

*Skimmed milk soft cheese makes a delicious, high-protein topping to
fruit and can be flavoured with any kind of fruit juice. Melon and
strawberries make a wonderful, sweet combination, but if they are out
of season try improvising with other fruit.*

Preparation time: 25 mins
Serves 4

METHOD

1. Scoop the melon flesh into small balls with a spoon.

2. Slice the strawberries and mix with the melon balls.
Refrigerate to chill.

3. In a blender, mix the quark with the orange juice and vanilla
essence until smooth.

4. Serve the fruit salad with a topping of the quark mixture.

Illustrated opposite

FILLED MELON SALAD

INGREDIENTS

2 Ogen melons
1 orange
6oz (175g) raspberries
juice of 1 lime

•

NUTRITION PROFILE

*This high-fibre fruit salad is a good source
of Vitamins A and C and iron. It is fat-
free and low in calories.*

• Per portion •
Carbohydrate: 17.8g
Protein: 3.2g   **Fibre:** 6.3g
Fat: --   **Calories:** 85

*This attractive dessert of fruit-filled melon halves makes a light and
clean-tasting end to a meal. Small Ogen melons from Israel have richly
flavoured green flesh, which combines well with the sweet raspberry and
orange flavours. Adding lime juice not only increases the vitamin
content but also adds a refreshing tang.*

Preparation time: 15 mins (plus chilling time)
Serves 4

METHOD

1. Cut the melons in half and discard the seeds. Scoop out a little
of the flesh from the centre of each half.

2. Peel and segment the orange, reserving all the juice. Cut the
segments in half.

3. Divide the raspberries and orange pieces between the melon
halves, then sprinkle with a little lime juice. Refrigerate
and serve chilled.

Illustrated opposite

Clockwise from top left: **Golden fruit salad** (*see p. 21*); **Melon and strawberry salad with creamy orange topping** (*see above*);
Filled melon salad (*see above*).

LATE SUMMER SALAD

INGREDIENTS
1 William pear
1 crisp red dessert apple
8oz (250g) red plums
8oz (250g) greengages
¼ pint (150ml) apple or pear juice

GARNISH
1 orange, thinly sliced
•

NUTRITION PROFILE
This fat-free, low-calorie dessert is a good source of Vitamin C.
• Per portion •
Carbohydrate: 24.3g
Protein: 1.2g Fibre: 4.5g
Fat: -- Calories: 100

Fruit salads can, of course, be made at any time of year, but those made with late-summer orchard fruit make a pleasant and inexpensive change from tropical versions.

Preparation time: 15 mins (plus chilling time)
Serves 4

METHOD
1. Wash the fruit but do not peel.

2. Core and chop the pear and apple into chunky pieces. Stone and chop the plums and greengages.

3. Mix the fruits together with the fruit juice in a serving bowl. Garnish with the orange slices, refrigerate and serve chilled.

Illustrated opposite

MIXED FRUIT SALAD IN SPICED YOGURT

INGREDIENTS
4oz (125g) black grapes
2 large bananas
1 peach
1 crisp green apple
7–8 fl oz (200–250ml) natural yogurt
2–3 tbsp (30–45ml) smetana (optional)
½ inch (1cm) freshly grated root ginger

GARNISH
ground cinnamon
•

NUTRITION PROFILE
A low-fat, low-calorie dessert, this salad is also a good source of Vitamin C and calcium.
• Per portion •
Carbohydrate: 23g
Protein: 3.5g Fibre: 2g
Fat: 0.7g Calories: 105

Yogurt is a wonderful ingredient – it is low in fat, its live enzymes ward off harmful bacteria in the digestive system, it makes a useful substitute for cream and it is easy to make. Here, the yogurt coating helps to preserve some of the more delicate vitamins that are destroyed when cut fruit is left exposed to the air. Use this tempting recipe as a dessert or a healthy breakfast dish.

Preparation time: 15 mins
Serves 4

METHOD
1. Halve and deseed the grapes.

2. Peel and chop the bananas. Stone and chop the peach. Core and chop the apple.

3. Mix all the fruit with the natural yogurt, smetana (if used) and ginger in a serving bowl. Sprinkle with cinnamon just before serving.

Illustrated opposite

Clockwise from top left: **Mixed fruit salad in spiced yogurt** (see above); **Stuffed kiwi fruit** (see p. 26); **Fresh date and mango platter** (see p. 27); **Late summer salad** (see above).

STUFFED KIWI FRUIT

INGREDIENTS

4 kiwi fruit
3oz (75g) curd cheese
1–2 tsp (5–10ml) chopped mint leaves
4 large strawberries, hulled

GARNISH
sprigs of fresh mint

•

NUTRITION PROFILE

This low-calorie dessert is a good source of Vitamin C.

• Per portion •
Carbohydrate: 7.9g
Protein: 2.5g   Fibre: 0.9g
Fat: 3.4g   Calories: 70

The kiwi fruit, a good source of Vitamin C, is often confined to garnishing. But filled with curd cheese and decorated with mint and strawberries, it makes a light, refreshing and nutritious dessert.

Preparation time: 25 mins
Serves 4

METHOD

1. Slice a third off the top of each kiwi fruit, put to one side and prepare the remaining two thirds (see below).

2. Scoop out the kiwi fruit flesh, chop or mash it, then mix with the curd cheese and mint.

3. Pile the cheese mixture back into the kiwi fruit.

4. Carefully peel the remaining pieces of kiwi fruit, cut into rings, then halve. Halve the strawberries.

5. Arrange the strawberry and kiwi slices on top of each stuffed kiwi fruit. Garnish with sprigs of mint and serve on individual plates.

Illustrated on page 25

STUFFING A KIWI FRUIT

Fruit often makes an attractive and unusual way of serving a dish as well as providing a nutritious ingredient in the recipe itself. Lemons and oranges are often used as cases for sorbets, and melons and pineapples as cases for fruit salads. Kiwi fruits make dainty and unusual containers for a light dessert, but require careful handling because the skins are rather fragile.

1. Cut off the top third of the kiwi fruit and peel the lid.

2. Carefully scoop out the inside of the fruit with a small spoon. Fill with the cheese and mashed kiwi flesh mixture.

3. Arrange small pieces of kiwi fruit and strawberry halves in a pattern on top.

FRESH DATE ~ MANGO PLATTER

INGREDIENTS
8–10oz (250–300g) fresh dates
1 large mango or 2 small mangoes
1oz (25g) slivered almonds
1oz (25g) cashew nut pieces
•

NUTRITION PROFILE
This dessert is rich in Vitamins A and C and high in fibre.

• Per portion •
Carbohydrate: 40.8g
Protein: 3.5g **Fibre:** 9.7g
Fat: 6.5g **Calories:** 230

Mangoes contain an enzyme that aids digestion, and when combined with dates and nuts provide a good balance of vitamins and minerals. Choose mangoes that smell ripe and are fairly soft to touch, and handle them gently.

Preparation time: 10 mins   Cooking time: 7–10 mins
Serves 4

METHOD
1. Halve and stone the dates.

2. Peel the mango and slice the flesh coarsely, away from the stone. There should be about 1lb (500g) of flesh.

3. Lightly toast the nuts under a preheated grill for 2–3 minutes, or in a preheated moderate oven at Gas Mark 4, 350°F, 180°C for 7–10 minutes.

4. Arrange the mango and dates on 4 individual plates, and sprinkle with toasted nuts.

Illustrated on page 25

COTTAGE CHEESE ~ FRUIT PLATTER

INGREDIENTS
4oz (125g) green seedless grapes
2 passion fruit or 2 fresh figs, halved
4oz (125g) raspberries or redcurrants
4oz (125g) black cherries, blackberries
or black grapes
1 orange
1 star fruit
8oz (250g) cottage cheese

GARNISH
4 walnut halves
•

NUTRITION PROFILE
This dessert is a good source of fibre and protein and is rich in Vitamin B$_{12}$ and C.

• Per portion •
Carbohydrate: 15.8g
Protein: 10.1g **Fibre:** 5.2g
Fat: 4.1g **Calories:** 135

A beautiful way to present fruit, this dish is easy to prepare, provides a good balance of nutrients and can be made with any combination of exotic fruit. Star fruit has a delicate, sweet-sour flavour. It can be peeled, or not, as you prefer. To reduce the fat content further, use half-fat cottage cheese.

Preparation time: 20 mins
Serves 4

METHOD
1. Wash all the fruit, string the redcurrants, peel and slice the orange and slice the star fruit.

2. Divide the cottage cheese and pile in the centre of 4 individual plates. Arrange the fruit in attractive clusters around the cheese. For example, 4 grapes in a bunch, half a passion fruit or fig, 3 raspberries, 2 slices of star fruit, 2 cherries, 4 more grapes, 2 slices of orange, 4 raspberries, 2 cherries.

3. Decorate the cheese with walnut halves.

Illustrated on page 29

FRUIT ～ NUT SALAD

INGREDIENTS

8oz (250g) fresh pineapple, peeled
and chopped
1 peach, stoned and sliced
6oz (175g) seedless green grapes
2–3 satsumas, peeled and segmented
juice of 1 orange
1oz (25g) Brazil nuts, chopped

•

NUTRITION PROFILE

*This salad is rich in Vitamin C and
low in calories.*

• Per portion •
Carbohydrate: 19.2g
Protein: 1.7g **Fibre:** 2.3g
Fat: 3.9g **Calories:** 115

*A small quantity of nuts adds protein and a new texture to a fruit salad.
Nuts are best bought whole and then chopped, since broken pieces do
not keep as well. To increase the protein content, try serving this dish
with natural yogurt or smetana.*

Preparation time: 15 mins
Serves 4

METHOD

1. Wash and prepare all the fruit and mix together in a
serving bowl.

2. Spoon over the orange juice.

3. Gently stir in the chopped nuts and serve immediately.

Illustrated opposite

TROPICAL SALAD

INGREDIENTS

1 pawpaw
8oz (250g) fresh dates, stoned
and sliced
2 bananas, peeled and sliced
juice of 1 lemon
2 tsp (10ml) clear honey
2 tbsp (30ml) grated creamed coconut

•

NUTRITION PROFILE

*This dessert is a good source of Vitamin C
and is low in fat and high in fibre.*

• Per portion •
Carbohydrate: 40.5g
Protein: 1.8g **Fibre:** 7.8g
Fat: 1.6g **Calories:** 180

*This rich, silky fruit salad gains its velvety texture from the coconut as
well as the smooth-fleshed fruits and honey. Pawpaw, or papaya,
similar to a mango, is beneficial to the digestive system and is yellow
when ripe. To ripen green fruit, leave in a warm place for a few days.*

Preparation time: 20 mins
Serves 4

METHOD

1. Halve the pawpaw, discarding the seeds. Scoop out the flesh
and chop.

2. Place the pawpaw, dates and bananas in a serving bowl.

3. Mix the lemon juice and honey together then stir into
the fruit.

4. Gently stir in the coconut.

Illustrated opposite

From top: **Cottage cheese and fruit platter** (*see p. 27*); **Tropical salad** (*see above*); **Fruit and nut salad** (*see above*);
Mixed fruit bowl with cheese platter and nuts (*see p. 30*).

MIXED FRUIT BOWL
WITH CHEESE PLATTER ᴬᴺᴰ NUTS

INGREDIENTS

CHEESE
3–4oz (75–125g) Camembert
3–4oz (75–125g) curd cheese or
Crowdie (fine-grain cottage cheese)
3–4oz (75–125g) Cheddar cheese

FRUIT AND NUTS
2 apples
2 nectarines
2 oranges
8oz (250g) fresh dates
8oz (250g) black or green grapes
8oz (250g) shelled mixed nuts

•

NUTRITION PROFILE

This provides a good source of Vitamins A,
B_2, B_{12} *and C, calcium and zinc.*

• Per portion •
Carbohydrate: 31g
Protein: 15.2g **Fibre:** 6.3g
Fat: 22.7g **Calories:** 385

A full platter of cheese, fruit and nuts is a relaxed way to end a meal and provides plenty of protein, vitamins and minerals. Choose low-fat cheeses, including some soft varieties such as curd cheese, which can be mixed with herbs before serving. Serve at least double the quantity of fruit to cheese, to keep the fat content down. The nuts can be served unshelled and the fruit left whole, if you prefer. Select them so that they provide plenty of contrast in shape and colour.

Preparation time: 10 mins
Serves 8

METHOD

1. Put spoonfuls of soft cheeses and slices of the hard cheese around the outside of a large platter.

2. Slice the apples and nectarines, peel and segment the oranges, halve and stone the dates and deseed the grapes.

3. Arrange slices of the fruit in between the portions of cheese.

4. Place the nuts in small clusters in the centre of the platter.

Illustrated on page 29

POACHED FRUIT

Easy to prepare and to digest, poached fruit can be made from
fresh or dried fruit. It makes a light but nutritious dessert,
served hot or chilled; whole or puréed; or as a fruit sauce, with
yogurt or smetana. Stewed fruit will keep for about 3 days in
the fridge.

SPICED PUREE WITH FRESH APPLE

INGREDIENTS

1lb (500g) cooking apples, peeled,
cored and sliced
6 cloves
juice of 1 orange
³/₄oz (20g) margarine
¼ pint (150ml) natural set yogurt

GARNISH
1 red crisp dessert apple

•

NUTRITION PROFILE

*This dessert is low in calories and is a good
source of Vitamins C and D and calcium.*

• Per portion •
Carbohydrate: 18g
Protein: 2.3g **Fibre:** 3g
Fat: 3.4g **Calories:** 110

*Fresh raw dessert apple adds a crisp dimension to the spicy cooking
apple – and both are low in calories and fat-free. Natural set yogurt
completes the balance of taste and nutrients in this simple recipe.*

Preparation time: 15 mins   Cooking time: 10 mins
Serves 4

METHOD

1. Place the apples with the cloves and orange juice in
a small pan.

2. Dot the margarine on top, and cover the apple mixture with
greaseproof paper and a lid. Cook very gently for 10 minutes
or until soft.

3. Purée in a blender or food processor, or sieve until smooth.

4. Place a few spoonfuls of purée in the centre of four individual
plates. Spoon the yogurt around the outside.

5. Core the dessert apple, cut into very thin wedges and arrange
on the top. Serve warm.

Illustrated on page 32

POACHED PEARS
WITH REDCURRANT SAUCE

INGREDIENTS

4 pears, peeled
½ pint (300ml) orange juice
1–2 tbsp (15–30ml) concentrated
apple juice
1 bay leaf

SAUCE
8oz (250g) redcurrants

•

NUTRITION PROFILE

*This extremely healthy, low-calorie dessert
is free from fat, high in fibre and a rich
source of Vitamin C.*

• Per portion •
Carbohydrate: 21.7g
Protein: 1g   **Fibre:** 8.1g
Fat: –   **Calories:** 90

*The delicate almond flavour of the bay leaf adds subtlety to the
contrasting sweetness of the pears and the sharpness of the redcurrant
sauce. To counteract the acidity of this simple dish, try serving with
natural yogurt or smetana.*

Preparation time: 30 mins (plus chilling time)
Cooking time: 20 mins
Serves 4

METHOD

1. Place the pears in a pan with the orange juice, concentrated
apple juice and bay leaf. Poach for 12–15 minutes, turning if
necessary. Cool.

2. For the sauce, place the redcurrants with 2–3 tbsp (30–45ml)
of the pear liquid in a saucepan and lightly cook for 3 minutes
(see below).

3. Spoon some sauce on to each serving plate and stand a pear in
the centre. Serve chilled.

Illustrated opposite

MAKING REDCURRANT SAUCE

*Redcurrants are an excellent source of fibre and Vitamin C and have always played an important role in
traditional cooking – in jellies, jams and sauces. A versatile and healthy redcurrant sauce can be made
without flour or sugar. It makes an excellent purée, which is worth sieving to make it smoother. If thick
enough, it can be used as a sugar-free spread. The sauce will keep 3–4 days in the fridge.*

1. Cook the redcurrants lightly in
2–3 tbsp (30–45ml) liquid for
3 minutes until the juices start to run.

2. Purée the cooked fruit mixture in a
blender or food processor until smooth.

3. Sieve the sauce to remove the seeds
and pith. If serving warm, heat gently.

From top: **Poached pears with redcurrant sauce** (*see above*); **Spiced fruit compote** (*see p. 34*);
Spiced purée with fresh apple (*see p. 31*).

SPICED FRUIT COMPOTE

INGREDIENTS

8oz (250g) mixed dried fruit salad (such
as prunes, apples, apricots, pears
and peaches)
6–8 cloves
2 inch (5cm) cinnamon stick
¼ tsp grated nutmeg

•

NUTRITION PROFILE

*This fat-free, high-fibre dessert is rich in
iron and Vitamin A and is low in calories.*

• Per portion •
Carbohydrate: 30.5g
Protein: 2g **Fibre:** 10g
Fat: –– **Calories:** 130

*Dried fruits are usually sun-dried to retain their natural sweetness,
vitamins and minerals. To plump them up, rinse, then cover with liquid
and leave to soak overnight. Use whole spices for flavouring, since the
ground ones tend to discolour the fruit.*

Preparation time: 5 mins (plus overnight soaking time)
Cooking time: 40–50 mins
Serves 4

METHOD

1. Soak the fruit salad overnight in plenty of hot or cold water.

2. Place the fruit with the soaking liquid and spices in a saucepan.
Bring to the boil, cover and simmer gently for 40–50 minutes.

3. Serve hot or cold.

Illustrated on page 32

HUNZA APRICOTS WITH CALVADOS

INGREDIENTS

8oz (250g) Hunza apricots
juice of 2 oranges
6 cardamom seeds
2 tbsp (30ml) Calvados

•

NUTRITION PROFILE

*Rich in iron and Vitamin A, this dessert
also provides plenty of fibre and is low in
calories and free from fat.*

• Per portion •
Carbohydrate: 28.5g
Protein: 3g **Fibre:** 15g
Fat: –– **Calories:** 135

*Hunza apricots are wild fruit that are sun-dried whole. When stewed,
they have a mellower flavour than the usual dried Turkish apricots and
produce a rich juice.*

Preparation time: 5 mins (plus overnight soaking time)
Cooking time: 30–40 mins
Serves 4

METHOD

1. Put the fruit in a bowl with the orange juice, cover with water
and soak overnight.

2. Transfer the apricots with their soaking liquid to a saucepan.
Then add the cardamom seeds. Bring to the boil, cover and
simmer for 30–40 minutes.

3. Add the Calvados and serve hot or cold.

Illustrated opposite

From top: **Kissel** (*see p. 36*); **Hunza apricots with Calvados** (*see above*); **Stewed ginger plums** (*see p. 36*).

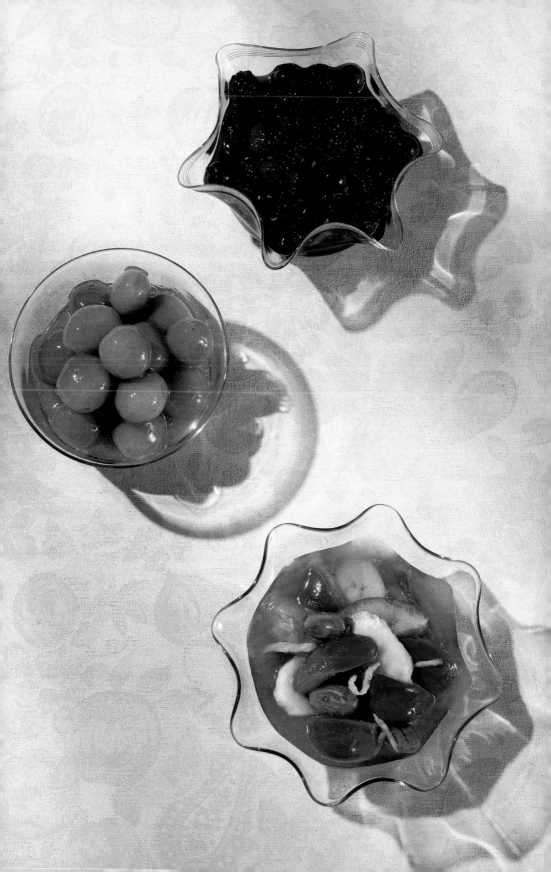

KISSEL

INGREDIENTS

4oz (125g) raspberries
8oz (250g) blackberries or
blackcurrants
1 tsp (5ml) arrowroot
4oz (125g) bilberries
1–2 tsp (5–10ml) clear honey

•

NUTRITION PROFILE

*Low-calorie and fat-free, this fruit dessert
is rich in Vitamins C and E, and
high in fibre.*

• Per portion •
Carbohydrate: 13.6g
Protein: 1.3g **Fibre:** 8.2g
Fat: –– **Calories:** 55

*Kissel is a traditional Russian dish of stewed fruit, thickened with
arrowroot. In this high-fibre version, I have kept some of the fruit whole
for a more interesting texture. Serve it with a spoonful of natural yogurt
or a little smetana.*

Preparation time: 15 mins (plus cooling time)
Cooking time: 5 mins
Serves 4

METHOD

1. In a blender, purée the raspberries and half the blackberries.
Sieve to remove the seeds. Place the purée in a saucepan.

2. Blend the arrowroot with 2 fl oz (50ml) water, and mix into the
fruit purée. Bring to the boil and simmer for 3 minutes.

3. Stir in the remaining blackberries and the bilberries. Sweeten
with honey to taste. Cook on a low heat for 2 minutes to soften
the whole fruits.

4. Serve cold.

Illustrated on page 35

STEWED GINGER PLUMS

INGREDIENTS

1lb (500g) cooking plums, stoned
and chopped
2 bananas, peeled and sliced
4oz (125g) raisins
½ tsp freshly grated root ginger

•

NUTRITION PROFILE

*This fruit dessert is rich in Vitamins B$_6$
and C. It is high in fibre and low in fat.*

• Per portion •
Carbohydrate: 41.9g
Protein: 1.7g **Fibre:** 5.8g
Fat: 0.2g **Calories:** 165

*Raisins and bananas lend sweetness to fresh cooking plums and
contribute extra vitamins and minerals. The ginger blends perfectly
with the fruity taste.*

Preparation time: 10 mins   Cooking time: 10 mins
Serves 4

METHOD

1. Mix the plums, bananas and raisins with the grated ginger.
Add 2 tbsp (30ml) water.

2. Cover and gently stew the fruit over a very low heat for 10
minutes or until just softened.

3. Serve hot or warm.

Illustrated on page 35

LAYERED AND ~ CRUNCHY PUDDINGS

These low-fat, high-fibre recipes are healthy versions of traditionally guilt-laden, rich desserts. They are substantial, nonetheless, so are best served at the end of a light meal.

SUMMER PUDDING

INGREDIENTS

6oz (175g) raspberries
4oz (125g) redcurrants
6oz (175g) blackcurrants
3 fl oz (75ml) red grape juice
4oz (125g) Swiss Vogel bread, without crusts

•

NUTRITION PROFILE

This pudding is low in fat and calories and contains plenty of fibre and protein. It is also a good source of iron, calcium and Vitamin C.

• Per portion •
Carbohydrate: 21.4g
Protein: 4g **Fibre:** 11.2g
Fat: 0.9g **Calories:** 105

This delicious traditional pudding is given a healthy, high-fibre slant here by using a mixed-grain Swiss bread and not overcooking the fruit. Make sure the bread is well moistened by the fruit juice, and push each layer right to the sides of the bowl, so that the pudding turns out whole. It works equally well with bilberries, loganberries or tayberries, and is excellent served with natural yogurt or smetana.

Preparation time: 30 mins (plus overnight standing time)
Serves 4

METHOD

1. Wash all the fruit and string the currants.

2. Place the fruit with the grape juice in a saucepan. Bring to the boil, then leave to cool.

3. Slice the bread thinly. Use one slice to line the base of a 1½ pint (900ml) pudding basin. Spoon over some fruit. Repeat layers of fruit and bread, ending with bread.

4. Put a plate or saucer with weights on the top and leave overnight. Turn out on to a rimmed plate and serve.

Illustrated on page 40

PAWPAW ~ LYCHEE PAVLOVA

INGREDIENTS

BASE
3 egg whites
4oz (125g) soft brown sugar
2 tbsp (30ml) cornmeal

TOPPING
1 pawpaw, peeled and finely chopped
4oz (125g) natural fromage frais

GARNISH
8 lychees, peeled, stoned and halved
1 lime, sliced

•

NUTRITION PROFILE

This low-fat dessert is a rich source of Vitamin C and protein.

• Per portion •
Carbohydrate: 48g
Protein: 10.2g   Fibre: 1.1g
Fat: 1.7g   Calories: 250

This luxurious version of pavlova is made with a low-sugar base. This means it will take longer to cook and is inevitably more sticky. If you prefer the traditional crisper meringue, you will need to add an extra 2oz (50g) of sugar. The fromage frais topping tastes rich but is low in fat. For a plainer alternative, try just fresh fruit or a little natural yogurt.

Preparation time: 25 mins   Cooking time: 1½–1¾ hours
Serves 4–6

METHOD

1. For the base, combine the egg whites, sugar and cornmeal to make the meringue mixture (see below).

2. Spoon in a 6 inch (15cm) round on a baking sheet, lined with greaseproof paper or non-stick baking parchment. Form a hollow in the centre and at the side edges.

3. Bake in a preheated oven at Gas Mark 2, 300°F, 150°C for 1½–1¾ hours. Cool under a cloth. Then carefully remove the baking paper.

4. Fold the finely chopped pawpaw into the fromage frais and spread over the base.

5. Decorate with lychees and lime and serve cold.

Illustrated on page 40

MAKING A PAVLOVA

A pavlova is a meringue-based dish, created for the ballet dancer Pavlova when she visited Australia in the 1930's. This version is made with brown sugar and fromage frais, instead of white sugar and cream. The less sugar you use, the softer and stickier the meringue becomes, although it still tastes just as good.

1. Beat 3 egg whites in a large bowl until stiff but not dry.

2. Gradually add 2oz (50g) of sugar, whisking all the time. Then whisk in the remaining 2oz (50g) sugar.

3. Fold in the cornmeal thoroughly. Spoon the mixture on to a lined baking sheet, making a meringue nest.

STRAWBERRY CHEESECAKE

INGREDIENTS

BASE
2oz (50g) margarine
2 tbsp (30ml) pear and apple spread
1 egg yolk
2oz (50g) self-raising wholemeal flour

FILLING
8oz (250g) skimmed milk soft
cheese (quark)
2 eggs
$\frac{1}{4}$ pint (150ml) smetana or
natural yogurt

GARNISH
8oz (250g) strawberries
•

NUTRITION PROFILE

This high-protein dessert is rich in Vitamins A, B_{12}, C, D and E, and is a good source of calcium.

• Per portion •
Carbohydrate: 17.5g
Protein: 9.9g **Fibre:** 1.2g
Fat: 10.1g **Calories:** 200

This baked cheesecake, which sets when cooked, is made from a healthy mixture of low-fat soft cheese, eggs and smetana. Uncooked versions often rely on double cream or full-fat cheese for texture. For an alternative healthy recipe that requires no cooking, use wholemeal digestive biscuits and margarine for the base, and mix honey with curd cheese and yogurt for the filling. Chill in the fridge for an hour and decorate with fresh summer fruit.

Preparation time: 45 mins   Cooking time: 45 mins
Serves 6–8

METHOD

1. For the base, cream together the margarine and the pear and apple spread in a bowl. Beat in the egg yolk and flour. Spread into a greased 7 inch (18cm) loose-based cake tin.

2. Bake in a preheated oven at Gas Mark 5, 375°F, 190°C for 15 minutes.

3. Beat the filling ingredients together in a bowl.

4. Pour on to the sponge base. Lower the oven temperature to Gas Mark 4, 350°F, 180°C and bake for 30 minutes. Leave to cool then remove from the tin.

5. For the topping, purée 4oz (125g) strawberries in a blender or food processor until smooth. Sieve to remove seeds. When the cheesecake is cold, spread with the strawberry purée.

6. Slice the remaining strawberries and use to garnish the cheesecake.

Illustrated on page 40

GRAPE AND PECAN GALETTE

INGREDIENTS

BASE
4oz (125g) dried dates, stoned
and chopped
3 egg whites
4oz (125g) pecan nuts

TOPPING
6oz (175g) white grapes, deseeded
1/4 pint (150ml) natural yogurt

•

NUTRITION PROFILE

*This pudding contains useful amounts of
iron and calcium.*

• Per portion •
Carbohydrate: 32.2g
Protein: 8.3g **Fibre:** 3.4g
Fat: 13.1g **Calories:** 265

*The light date and nut base of this dish is rather like a soft meringue and
perfectly complements the fresh grape topping. You can deseed grapes
by cutting them in half and removing the pips with the tip of a sharp
knife. Pecans, probably best known because of the famous American
Pecan Pie are rather like walnuts in appearance, but have a smooth,
glossy shell and a mild, sweet flavour. They also contain less fat than
walnuts. For the best results, make this dessert on the day it is to be
eaten.*

Preparation time: 1 hour   Cooking time: 30 mins
Serves 4

METHOD

1. Place the dates in a saucepan, then cover with a little water.
Cook gently for 10–15 minutes, beating well into a thick purée.
Leave until cold.

2. Whisk the egg whites until stiff. Whip in the date purée.

3. Reserving 8 pecan halves for the decoration, and a few more to
mix with the yogurt later, grind 2oz (50g) pecan nuts in a
blender, food processor or nut mill and fold into the egg
white mixture.

4. Line a baking sheet with greaseproof paper or non-stick baking
parchment. Spread the mixture in a 7 inch (18cm) round on the
baking sheet.

5. Bake in a preheated oven at Gas Mark 4, 350°F, 180°C for 30
minutes. Cover with a cloth and leave to cool.

6. Chop the grapes and remaining pecan nuts (but not the halves
reserved for decoration). Mix with
the yogurt.

7. Spoon the grape mixture over the base. Decorate with the
reserved pecan halves and serve immediately.

Illustrated on page 43

From top: **Strawberry cheesecake** (*see p. 39*); **Pawpaw and lychee pavlova** (*see p. 38*);
Summer pudding (*see p. 37*).

NECTARINE AND HAZELNUT CRUNCH

INGREDIENTS

2oz (50g) oatmeal
2oz (50g) hazelnuts, coarsely chopped
1 tsp (5ml) grated orange rind
3 nectarines, peeled, stoned and sliced
juice of 1 orange

•

NUTRITION PROFILE

This is a good source of Vitamins C and E.

• Per portion •
Carbohydrate: 21.3g
Protein: 3.3g **Fibre:** 3.7g
Fat: 5.6g **Calories:** 145

This is an upside-down dessert. The crunchy nut mixture keeps the fruit moist and protects it as it bakes. Hazelnuts make an excellent topping for a number of sweet and savoury dishes when chopped or crushed. They are lower in saturated fat than other nuts, but extremely high in Vitamin E. Try serving this dish with natural yogurt or smetana.

Preparation time: 30 mins   Cooking time: 30 mins
Serves 4

METHOD

1. Place the oatmeal on a baking sheet and toast in a preheated oven at Gas Mark 4, 350°F, 180°C for 8–10 minutes. Leave to cool, then mix well with the hazelnuts and orange rind.

2. Lightly grease a 7 inch (18cm) flan tin. Place a layer of nectarines over the base. Sprinkle half the nut and oatmeal mixture over the top, then arrange a second layer of nectarines using the remaining slices. Cover with the remaining nut and oatmeal and press down well.

3. Pour the orange juice carefully over the top, making sure that all the dry mixture is well moistened (squeeze another orange if necessary).

4. Bake in a preheated oven at Gas Mark 4, 350°F, 180°C for 30 minutes. Cool, then turn out of the tin. Warm through before serving.

Illustrated opposite

From top: **Nectarine and hazelnut crunch** (*see above*); **Grape and pecan galette** (*see p. 41*);
Cherry and sunflower scone (*see p. 44*).

CHERRY ~ SUNFLOWER SCONE

INGREDIENTS

SCONE BASE
4oz (125g) wholemeal flour
1½ tsp (7.5ml) baking powder
½ tsp ground cinnamon
1oz (25g) muscovado sugar
1oz (25g) sunflower seeds
1oz (25g) margarine
1 egg, beaten

TOPPING
1lb (500g) black cherries, stoned
6 fl oz (175ml) natural set yogurt

•

NUTRITION PROFILE

*A good source of calcium and Vitamins A,
C, D and E, this dish also contains a small
amount of Vitamin B$_{12}$.*

• Per portion •
Carbohydrate: 30.5g
Protein: 5.3g Fibre: 2.3g
Fat: 6.9g Calories: 205

*This unusual scone recipe is lower in fat and sugar than many
conventional biscuit or sponge bases. The sunflower seeds add a
crunchy texture, nutty flavour and vitamins.*

Preparation time: 50 mins   Cooking time: 12 mins
Serves 6–8

METHOD

1. For the base, stir the flour, baking powder, cinnamon, sugar
and sunflower seeds together in a bowl. Rub in the margarine. Stir
in the egg and 1 tbsp (15ml) water. Form into a soft dough.

2. Roll out to a 7 inch (18cm) round. Place on a lined baking
sheet and bake in a preheated oven at Gas Mark 7, 425°F, 220°C
for 12 minutes. Leave to cool.

3. For the topping, purée half the cherries in a blender or food
processor until quite smooth.

4. Spread the cherry purée over the scone base. Carefully spread
the yogurt on top and decorate with the remaining cherry halves.

Illustrated on page 43

LAYERED MUESLI PUDDING

INGREDIENTS

3oz (75g) jumbo oats
3oz (75g) oat flakes
1½oz (40g) sunflower seeds
1½oz (40g) walnuts, chopped
2–3 bananas, peeled and sliced
8oz (250g) fresh dates, stoned
and chopped
½ pint (300ml) natural yogurt

•

NUTRITION PROFILE

*High in fibre and protein, this dessert is a
good source of Vitamins B$_1$, B$_6$, C and E,
folic acid, zinc, calcium, magnesium
and iron.*

• Per portion •
Carbohydrate: 69.4g
Protein: 13.3g Fibre: 8.9g
Fat: 14.6g Calories: 450

*This highly nutritious pudding makes a good follow-up to a light meal.
If it follows a heavier main course, the quantities given will serve 6.
Serve in individual glasses.*

Preparation time: 30 mins (plus 2 hours' standing time)
Cooking time: 8–10 mins
Serves 4

METHOD

1. Mix together the jumbo oats, oat flakes, seeds and nuts. Spread
out on a baking sheet and toast lightly in a preheated oven at Gas
Mark 4, 350°F, 180°C for 8–10 minutes.

2. Arrange a layer of bananas and dates in the base of four glasses.
Cover with the toasted cereal mix, then spoon over a layer
of yogurt. Continue to add layers, finishing with yogurt. Sprinkle
a little cereal on top.

3. Allow to stand for 2 hours before serving.

Illustrated on page 46

BILBERRY TRIFLE

INGREDIENTS

SPONGE
2 eggs
2oz (50g) pear and apple spread
2oz (50g) wholemeal flour

FILLING
8oz (250g) bilberries, destalked
juice of 1 large orange

CUSTARD
1 tbsp (15ml) cornmeal
¼ pint (150ml) skimmed milk
4 tbsp (60ml) natural set yogurt
1 tbsp (15ml) clear honey (optional)

GARNISH
1oz (25g) toasted, flaked almonds

•

NUTRITION PROFILE

This trifle is a good source of Vitamins B₁₂, C, D, and E and of iron and calcium.

This trifle is a good source of Vitamins B_{12}, C, D, and E and of iron and calcium.

• Per portion •
Carbohydrate: 35.6g
Protein: 8.6g   **Fibre:** 2.1g
Fat: 6.6g   **Calories:** 230

This delicious trifle, flavoured with the tangy taste of bilberries, is substantial yet relatively low in fat. If bilberries are not available, try using black- or redcurrants. The fruit and the pear and apple spread sweeten the dish naturally, but if you like extra sweetness, add a little honey to the custard, instead of refined sugar.

Preparation time: 50 mins   Cooking time: 25–30 mins
Serves 4–6

METHOD

1. For the sponge, beat the eggs and pear and apple spread in a bowl until light and thick and the whisk leaves a trail in the mixture. Fold in the flour.

2. Spoon the mixture into a greased 6 inch (15cm) cake tin. Bake in a preheated oven at Gas Mark 4, 350°F, 180°C for 25–30 minutes.

3. Leave to cool, then slice in half to make a sandwich.

4. For the filling, place the bilberries in a saucepan with the orange juice and gently simmer for 2–3 minutes. In a blender or food processor, purée half the mixture.

5. Fill the sponge with the purée, then chop the sponge sandwich into small pieces and put in a serving bowl or individual dishes.

6. Sprinkle the remaining berries on top.

7. For the custard, blend the cornmeal with the skimmed milk in a saucepan. Bring to the boil and cook gently for 5 minutes, stirring constantly. Cool, then add nearly all the yogurt. Sweeten with a little honey if desired and spread the custard over the trifle.

8. Spoon the remaining yogurt on top and garnish with the almonds.

Illustrated on page 46

CHESTNUT AND CAROB SHORTBREAD
WITH APRICOTS

INGREDIENTS

SHORTBREAD
3oz (75g) dried chestnuts
3oz (75g) margarine
1oz (25g) brown sugar
4oz (125g) wholemeal flour
2 tbsp (30ml) carob flour

FILLING
8oz (250g) apricots, halved and stoned
1 tsp (5ml) arrowroot
2 tbsp (30ml) smetana

GARNISH
4 fresh apricots, sliced
•

NUTRITION PROFILE

*This dessert is rich in Vitamins A, D and E
and contains magnesium and iron.*

• Per portion •
Carbohydrate: 31.3g
Protein: 3.6g   **Fibre:** 3.5g
Fat: 11.1g   **Calories:** 235

*The chestnuts and carob provide the sweetness and help to keep the
shortbread moist. For the best topping, choose good, ripe apricots,
which are an excellent source of iron. If they are not in season, use
unsweetened, canned apricots, or dried apricots. Any remaining
cooked chestnuts can be frozen and used later in a cake or muesli dish,
or in a savoury nut loaf or pâté. 2–3oz (50–75g) dried weight will
make 4–6oz (125–175g) reconstituted cooked weight.*

Preparation time: 1 hour   Cooking time: 15–20 mins
Serves 6–8

METHOD

1. For the shortbread, place the chestnuts in a saucepan and add
plenty of water to cover. Bring to the boil and simmer for 35–40
minutes until fairly well cooked. Drain and weigh out 4oz (125g)
chestnuts (you may have a few left over), then grind to a powder
in a food processor or grinder.

2. Cream together the margarine and the sugar in a bowl.

3. Mix in the chestnut mixture and the wholemeal and
carob flours.

4. Divide the mixture between two 7 inch (18cm) greased and
floured sandwich tins. Mark the shortbread into 8 sections. Bake
in a preheated oven at Gas Mark 5, 375°F, 190°C for 15–20
minutes or until crisp.

5. Turn out the rounds and cool on wire racks.

6. For the topping, place the 8oz (250g) apricots in a saucepan
with 1 tbsp (15ml) water and simmer for 5 minutes. Cool slightly,
then purée in a blender or food processor. Return the purée to
the saucepan.

7. Dissolve the arrowroot in 1 tbsp (15ml) water and mix into the
apricot purée. Bring to the boil to thicken the sauce, stirring
continuously. Leave to cool and then stir in the smetana.

8. Spread the purée over one of the rounds of shortbread. Place
the second round on top, garnish with slices of apricot, cut into 8
sections and serve.

Illustrated opposite

Clockwise from top left: **Bilberry trifle** (*see p. 45*); **Layered muesli pudding** (*see p. 44*);
Chestnut and carob shortbread with apricots (*see above*).

KIWI AND PASSION FRUIT CAKE

INGREDIENTS

BASE
1½oz (40g) wholemeal breadcrumbs
1oz (25g) rolled oats
2oz (50g) wholemeal flour
1½oz (40g) ground almonds
¼ tsp almond essence
1½oz (40g) margarine

TOPPING
8oz (250g) ricotta cheese
8 fl oz (250ml) natural set yogurt
2 passion fruit
1 kiwi fruit, peeled and sliced

•

NUTRITION PROFILE

This high-protein cake is a good source of Vitamins A, C and D, also calcium and magnesium.

• Per portion •
Carbohydrate: 16.1g
Protein: 10g   **Fibre:** 3.5g
Fat: 17.3g   **Calories:** 255

The crisp, crumbly, low-fat base of this dish complements the smooth texture of the ricotta and yogurt topping and the slightly sharp fruit flavours. Sweet, juicy kiwi fruit slices make an attractive decoration. Kiwi fruit originally came from China, and are also known as Chinese gooseberries. They are now grown chiefly in New Zealand. They store well in a cool place and can be frozen successfully. You can eat the skin as well as the seeds and flesh, but they are usually peeled. The delicate flavour and colour of the kiwi fruit are complemented by the fragrance of the passion fruit. Choose the large, dark passion fruit when buying. Natural set yogurt and ricotta cheese make a creamy-tasting but low-fat combination for the topping.

Preparation time: 35 mins (plus overnight standing time)
Cooking time: 15–20 mins
Serves 6

METHOD

1. For the base, mix all the ingredients together and press into a loose-based 6 inch (15cm) flan tin.

2. Bake in a preheated oven at Gas Mark 5, 375°F, 190°C for 15–20 minutes. Leave to cool.

3. For the topping, mix the ricotta cheese and set yogurt in a blender. Spoon on to the base and leave to set overnight.

4. Scoop out the flesh of the passion fruit and spread it over the top of the cheesecake. Decorate with slices of kiwi fruit.

Illustrated opposite

Kiwi and passion fruit cake (*see above*).

BAKED PUDDINGS

"Casseroled" desserts are a warming, filling way to end a meal and when based on fruit they can be surprisingly low in fat and sugar, and inexpensive. Although designed to be served piping hot, many of these puddings are equally good served cold, if you have any left over.

PINEAPPLE PUDDING

INGREDIENTS

2oz (50g) margarine
1oz (25g) clear honey
7oz (200g) skimmed milk soft cheese (quark)
1 egg, separated
1oz (25g) ground almonds
1oz (25g) rice flour
1 tsp (5ml) grated orange rind
12oz (375g) fresh pineapple

•

NUTRITION PROFILE

High in protein, this pudding also contains a good supply of Vitamins A, C, D and E, and some B$_{12}$.

• Per portion •
Carbohydrate: 22.5g
Protein: 11g **Fibre:** 2.1g
Fat: 15.1g **Calories:** 270

This light, creamy fruit pudding uses skimmed milk soft cheese, well moistened with almonds and egg. It is an excellent cheese for baking, but its lack of fat can make it dry. To reduce the sugar content, you could make a date purée (see Pineapple and Carob Cream, p. 84), to use instead of honey.

Preparation time: 25 mins Cooking time: 50 mins
Serves 4

METHOD

1. Cream the margarine and honey together in a bowl until light and fluffy.

2. Gradually beat in the skimmed milk soft cheese and egg yolk.

3. Stir in the almonds, rice flour and orange rind. Roughly chop the pineapple and add to the mixture.

4. Beat the egg white until stiff and then fold into the pineapple mixture.

5. Spoon the mixture into a greased 6 inch (15cm) loose-based fluted flan tin. Bake in a preheated oven at Gas Mark 5, 375°F, 190°C for 50 minutes. Leave to cool slightly and then refrigerate. Serve cold with some natural yogurt.

Illustrated on page 52

ORANGE AND RAISIN GRANOLA

INGREDIENTS

BASE
6 oranges (or 4 oranges and 2 pink grapefruit)
6oz (175g) seeded raisins

TOPPING
8oz (250g) muesli
2 tsp (10ml) ground cinnamon
2 tsp (10ml) sunflower oil
2 tbsp (30ml) malt extract

•

NUTRITION PROFILE

This high-protein, high-fibre pudding is a good source of Vitamin C, calcium, iron, copper, magnesium, zinc and folic acid.

• Per portion •
Carbohydrate: 87.4g
Protein: 9.9g   Fibre: 10.2g
Fat: 7.3g   Calories: 450

Granola, traditionally a baked cereal made from a muesli base and sweetened with oil and malt, is here used as a highly nutritious crumble topping.

Preparation time: 30 mins (plus 1 hour soaking time)
Cooking time: 20–25 mins
Serves 4

METHOD

1. Peel and segment the oranges (and grapefruit if using), carefully reserving the juice.

2. Place the segments in a small ovenproof dish. Add the raisins and the orange juice. Leave to soak for 1 hour.

3. For the topping, mix the muesli and cinnamon together. Stir the oil and malt extract together, then combine with the muesli. Spoon this over the oranges.

4. Bake in a preheated oven at Gas Mark 5, 375°F, 190°C for 20–25 minutes or until the topping is slightly browned.

Illustrated on page 52

PEAR AND PINE NUT PUDDING

INGREDIENTS

BASE
1½lb (750g) Conference pears
2oz (50g) sultanas
juice and rind of ½ lemon

TOPPING
2oz (50g) wholemeal flour
2oz (50g) pine nuts
1oz (25g) soft brown sugar
1 tsp (5ml) ground ginger
½ tsp ground cinnamon
4 fl oz (125ml) smetana

•

NUTRITION PROFILE

This pudding is high in fibre and a good source of Vitamin C and copper.

• Per portion •
Carbohydrate: 46.4g
Protein: 5.4g   Fibre: 7g
Fat: 10.8g   Calories: 285

This light, nutty crumble with its smetana topping complements the taste and texture of the sweet fruit filling and contributes fibre and vitamins.

Preparation time: 25 mins   Cooking time 15–20 mins
Serves 4–6

METHOD

1. Slice and core the pears, mix with the sultanas and lemon juice.

2. Fill a 1½ pint (900ml) ovenproof dish with the slices.

3. For the topping, mix together the flour, pine nuts, sugar, spices and lemon rind. Sprinkle over the fruit.

4. Mix the smetana with 1 tbsp (15ml) water. Pour this over the top of the pudding.

5. Bake in a preheated oven at Gas Mark 5, 375°F, 190°C for 15–20 minutes. Serve warm.

Illustrated on page 52

PLUM CHARLOTTE

INGREDIENTS

8–10 slices of fruit bread
2 tsp (10ml) concentrated apple juice
2 tsp (10ml) malt extract
1lb (500g) red plums, halved
and stoned
1–2 tbsp (15–30ml) clear
honey (optional)
¼ tsp ground mixed spice

•

NUTRITION PROFILE

*This low-fat dessert is a good source of iron
and calcium.*

• Per portion •
Carbohydrate: 56.4g
Protein: 5.6g   Fibre: 3.9g
Fat: 2.6g   Calories: 255

The concentrated fruit juice and malt extract (sometimes called barley syrup) sweeten both the bread and the plums. Plums are in season in late summer and early autumn. There are many different types: they come with red, black, blue, yellow or green skins; large or small; round or oval; sweet or sour. Plums make wonderful jams, jellies, sauces, purées, mousses and soufflés, but the skin can leave a bitter taste when cooked, so it's often best to peel them. They are also delicious used whole or halved in pies, tarts and flans. As you get used to using less sugar, you may not need to sweeten the plums with honey. Some natural yogurt or smetana will go well with this dessert.

Preparation time: 30 mins   Cooking time: 50–60 mins
Serves 4–5

METHOD

1. Cut the crusts off the fruit bread.

2. Mix together the concentrated apple juice and malt extract. Spread a little on one side of each slice of bread.

3. Lightly grease a 1½ pint (900ml) round ovenproof dish.

4. Cut one slice of bread to fit the base. Then slice the remaining pieces to overlap all around the sides, sticky side outwards. Leave some pieces for the top.

5. Place the plums in a saucepan with the honey and mixed spice and lightly poach for 4 minutes until just softening.

6. Press the plums into the centre of the bread-lined dish. Top with the remaining bread, sticky side down. Cover with foil.

7. Bake in a preheated oven at Gas Mark 5, 375°F, 190°C for 50–60 minutes.

8. Turn out and serve hot with yogurt or smetana.

Illustrated opposite

From top: **Pineapple pudding** (*see p.* 50); **Orange and raisin granola** (*see p.* 51); **Pear and pine nut pudding** (*see p.51*); Plum charlotte (*see above*).

GOOSEBERRY ~ BANANA COBBLER

INGREDIENTS

BASE
8oz (250g) gooseberries, topped and tailed
1 tsp (5ml) concentrated apple juice
2 ripe bananas, peeled and sliced

TOPPING
2oz (50g) wholemeal flour
2oz (50g) cornmeal
¼ tsp salt
½ tsp baking powder
1 tsp (5ml) sunflower oil
1 egg
2 fl oz (50ml) milk

•

NUTRITION PROFILE
This dish is a good source of Vitamins B₁₂, C, D and E.

• Per portion •
Carbohydrate: 33.7g
Protein: 4.7g   Fibre: 5.1g
Fat: 6.1g   Calories: 205

The sweet and sharp fruit combination makes an excellent sugar-free base for this quick, easy, and delicious pudding. Gooseberries become sweet and gooey when cooked with bananas and concentrated apple juice, so there is no need for added sugar.

Preparation time: 25 mins   Cooking time 30 mins
Serves 4

METHOD

1. Place the gooseberries in a saucepan with 1–2 tbsp (15–30ml) water and the concentrated apple juice and stew for 5 minutes.

2. Add the bananas to the gooseberries. Transfer to a small ovenproof dish.

3. For the topping, mix together the wholemeal flour, cornmeal, salt and baking powder in a bowl. Beat the oil, egg and milk together and make the cobbler dough (see below).

4. Roll out the dough to about ½ inch (1cm) thick, and cut into small rounds. Arrange attractively on top of the fruit (see below).

5. Bake in a preheated oven at Gas Mark 4, 350°F, 180°C for 30 minutes.

Illustrated opposite

MAKING A COBBLER

A cobbler, an American idea, can either be made of a thick dough which is cut into shapes, or from a thin batter which is simply poured on to the dish. It forms a light, golden crust – a lovely alternative to a pastry or crumble topping.

1. Mix the dry and liquid ingredients separately, then combine to make a stiff dough.

2. Roll out the dough to ½ inch (1cm) thickness and cut into small rounds using a scone cutter.

3. Arrange the cobbler rounds attractively on top of the prepared filling. Bake immediately.

From top: **Gooseberry and banana cobbler** (*see above*); **Peach and apple steamed pudding** (*see p. 56*).

PEACH ~AND~ APPLE STEAMED PUDDING

INGREDIENTS

DOUGH
½oz (15g) fresh yeast
3 fl oz (75ml) soya or skimmed milk, warmed
1 tsp (5ml) malt extract
6oz (175g) wholemeal flour
pinch salt
1 tbsp (15ml) sunflower oil
1 tbsp (15ml) soya flour

FILLING
6oz (175g) dried peaches, soaked
2oz (50g) currants, soaked
8oz (250g) cooking apples, peeled, cored and chopped

SAUCE
1–2 tsp (5–10ml) arrowroot

•
NUTRITION PROFILE

This high-fibre, low-fat dessert is rich in Vitamins A, B₁, C, E and niacin. It is also a good source of iron, magnesium and copper.

• Per portion •
Carbohydrate: 47g
Protein: 6.7g   **Fibre:** 8.9g
Fat: 2.7g   **Calories:** 235

A steamed, yeast crust makes a good light alternative to a suet pastry. Fresh yeast is available wherever there is an in-store bakery. Here, the sweetness of the dried fruit balances with the tart cooking apple and both are an excellent source of dietary fibre, and serving this pudding with natural yogurt or smetana will bring out the flavour of both. The fruity cooking liquor makes a delicious low-fat sauce.

Preparation time: 45 mins (plus overnight soaking time)   Cooking time: 2 hours
Serves 6

METHOD

1. For the dough, dissolve the yeast in the warm milk. Mix in the malt extract and leave to ferment for 5 minutes.

2. Mix the flour and salt. Add the fermented yeast mixture, then add the oil and soya flour.

3. Knead well to a soft dough. Leave to prove for 20 minutes.

4. Meanwhile for the filling, cook the peaches and currants together in their soaking liquid for 15–20 minutes until fairly soft. Add the cooking apple and cook for a further 5 minutes. Drain, reserving the liquor for the sauce.

5. Reserve one third of the dough and place on one side. Roll out the remaining dough into a large round. Arrange into a lightly greased 2 pint (1 litre) pudding basin so that the sides are covered up to the rim.

6. Spoon in the filling, cover with the reserved dough and seal the edges with water. Cover with greaseproof paper and a pudding cloth, tied securely.

7. Either steam for 2 hours, or steam for 10 minutes and pressure cook for 40 minutes.

8. For the sauce, dissolve the arrowroot in ½ pint (300ml) peach liquor. Bring to the boil and simmer for 4 minutes.

9. To serve the pudding, turn out, pour the sauce on top and serve.

Illustrated on page 55

FLANS, STRUDELS
AND
~
CREPES

The secret of healthy pastry and pancakes is to use wholemeal
flour, a fruit instead of a cream filling and natural sweetening.
They can be served hot or cold and lend themselves to any
number of different fruit fillings. Low-fat soft cheeses
combined with any sort of fruit make a delicious centre or
topping to a pastry or batter base.

ORANGE ~ APPLE FLAN
AND

INGREDIENTS

PASTRY
4oz (125g) wholemeal flour
pinch salt
½ tsp baking powder
2oz (50g) margarine
1 tsp (5ml) grated orange rind
2–3 tbsp (30–45ml) water

FILLING
4 dessert apples, peeled, cored
and chopped
8oz (250g) apricots, halved and stoned
2 oranges, peeled and sliced, with
juice reserved

GLAZE
2 tsp (10ml) clear honey
2 tsp (10 ml) concentrated apple juice

•

NUTRITION PROFILE

*This low-calorie dessert is a good source
of Vitamins A, B₁, C, D and E, and of
magnesium, iron and folic acid.*

• Per portion •
Carbohydrate: 28g
Protein: 3.5g **Fibre:** 4.9g
Fat: 7.2g **Calories:** 190

*This colourful flan is sweetened with apple juice concentrate. Serve it
warm with a little natural yogurt or smetana.*

Preparation time: 45 mins (plus 30 mins resting time)   Cooking time: 30 mins
Serves 6

METHOD

1. For the pastry, mix together the flour, salt and baking powder
in a bowl. Rub in the margarine until the mixture resembles fine
breadcrumbs. Add the orange rind and water and mix to a soft
dough. Leave to rest for 30 minutes.

2. Roll out and use to line a 7 inch (18cm) flan tin. Press down
well and prick the base. Bake in a preheated oven at Gas Mark 6,
400°F, 200°C for 5 minutes.

3. For the filling, place the apples and apricots with the orange
juice in a saucepan. Cover and poach for 10 minutes. Purée in a
blender or food processor.

4. Fill the flan case with purée. Cover with the slices of orange.
Bake for 20–25 minutes. Cool slightly.

5. For the glaze, mix the honey and concentrated apple juice
together. Brush over the fruit. Serve warm.

Illustrated on page 59

FRESH PEAR ~ RICOTTA FLAN

INGREDIENTS

PASTRY
4oz (125g) wholemeal flour
pinch salt
½ tsp baking powder
2oz (50g) soft margarine
1oz (25g) sesame seeds
2–3 tbsp (30–45ml) water

FILLING
4 pears, peeled, cored and chopped
7oz (200g) ricotta cheese
¼ tsp vanilla essence

TOPPING
1 pear
juice of ½ lemon
1–2 tsp (5–10ml) agar-agar flakes

•

NUTRITION PROFILE
*This flan is a good source of magnesium,
protein and fibre, and of Vitamins
A, B₁ and D.*

• Per portion •
Carbohydrate: 24.8g
Protein: 8.7g **Fibre:** 4.1g
Fat: 17.5g **Calories:** 285

Pastry is not thought of as a nutritious food, but using wholemeal flour instead of refined flour increases the protein, fibre, vitamin and mineral content. Wholemeal pastry has a denser texture than refined pastry, but adding a little baking powder will create a lighter effect. Here the sesame seeds and the wholemeal flour in the pastry give a good, crunchy base to the smooth fruit and cheese filling. Low-fat cheese is delicious with any fresh fruit and there is usually no need to add a sweetener, even when the fruit is cooked. The agar-agar, used for the glaze, is a vegetable gelatine-like product, available in powder or flake form. If you are using powder you will need less, as it is more concentrated than the flakes.

Preparation time: 1 hour (plus 30 mins resting time)
Cooking time: 15–20 mins
Serves 6

METHOD

1. For the pastry, mix together the flour, salt and baking powder in a bowl.

2. Rub in the margarine until the mixture resembles fine breadcrumbs. Mix in the sesame seeds.

3. Add the water and mix to a soft dough. Leave to rest for 30 minutes.

4. Roll out and use to line a 7 inch (18cm) flan tin. Prick the base. Bake in a preheated oven at Gas Mark 6, 400°F, 200°C for 15–20 minutes. Leave to cool.

5. For the filling, purée the pears in a blender or food processor, then spread over the pastry base.

6. Mix together the ricotta and vanilla essence in a blender. Spoon over the pear purée.

7. For the topping, thinly slice the pear, removing the core.

8. Make the lemon juice up to ¼ pint (150ml) with water in a saucepan. Add the agar-agar flakes and stir to dissolve. Bring to the boil and simmer for 5 minutes.

9. For the topping, either lightly poach the slices of pear before arranging on the flan, or arrange the raw fruit on the flan. Brush with the agar-agar glaze. Serve cold.

Illustrated opposite

APRICOT ~ GOOSEBERRY FLAN

INGREDIENTS

PASTRY
4oz (125g) wholemeal flour
pinch salt
½ tsp baking powder
2oz (50g) margarine
2–3 tbsp (30–45ml) water

ALMOND CREAM
4oz (125g) ground almonds
¼ pint (150ml) water
½ tsp ground ginger
3–4 drops almond essence
1 tbsp (15ml) clear honey (optional)

TOPPING
12oz (375g) fresh apricots, halved
and stoned
3–4oz (75–125g) dessert gooseberries,
topped and tailed

•

NUTRITION PROFILE

*This high-fibre flan is a good source of
Vitamins A, B₁, C, D and E, zinc,
calcium, iron and magnesium.*

• Per portion •
Carbohydrate: 34.4g
Protein: 9.1g **Fibre:** 9.5g
Fat: 24.1g **Calories:** 385

*Nut creams are a delicious and healthy alternative to confectioner's
custard, particularly as a base for fruit flans. Choose dessert
gooseberries for the topping – they are a good source of Vitamin C
and dietary fibre.*

Preparation time: 45 mins (plus 30 mins resting time)   Cooking time: 35 mins
Serves 4

METHOD

1. For the pastry, mix together the flour, salt and baking powder
in a bowl.

2. Rub in the margarine until the mixture resembles
fine breadcrumbs.

3. Sprinkle over the water and make into a firm dough. Leave to
rest for 30 minutes.

4. Roll out the dough and use to line a 7 inch (18cm) flan tin.
Press in firmly and prick well.

5. Bake in a preheated oven at Gas Mark 6, 400°F, 200°C
for 5 minutes.

6. For the almond cream filling, mix all the ingredients together.
Sweeten with honey if necessary. Spoon the filling into
the flan case.

7. For the topping, place 8oz (250g) apricots on top of the almond
cream around the edge of the flan. Fill the centre with
gooseberries. Reduce the oven temperature to Gas Mark 5, 375°F,
190°C and bake for 25–30 minutes.

8. Place the remaining apricots in a saucepan with 1 tbsp (15ml)
water. Simmer for 5 minutes. Transfer to a blender or food
processor and purée until smooth.

9. When the flan is cooked, carefully spoon over the apricot
purée. Serve warm.

Illustrated on page 59

PRUNE STRUDEL

INGREDIENTS

DOUGH
4oz (125g) wholemeal flour
1 egg yolk
1 tbsp (15ml) sunflower oil
6 tbsp (90ml) warm water

FILLING
8oz (250g) pitted prunes , soaked
$\frac{1}{4}$ tsp ground allspice
$\frac{1}{4}$ tsp vanilla essence
2 tbsp (30ml) port
4oz (125g) walnuts, chopped

GLAZE
$\frac{1}{2}$oz (15g) butter, melted
2 tsp (10ml) clear honey
2 tsp (10ml) concentrated apple juice
•

NUTRITION PROFILE

High in fibre, this pudding is also rich in Vitamins A, B_1, B_2, B_6, D and E, and in magnesium, iron, zinc and folic acid.

• Per portion •
Carbohydrate: 34.1g
Protein: 5.3g **Fibre:** 8.6g
Fat: 16.9g **Calories:** 315

Strudels are useful pastry desserts, since they are quite low in fat. If you make an eggless dough, add a little soya flour and extra oil. You can leave out the butter coating, but the strudel will not brown so well.

Preparation time: 1 hour (plus overnight soaking time)   Cooking time: 35 mins
Serves 6

METHOD

1. Place the flour, egg yolk, oil and warm water in a bowl and mix together. Make the strudel dough (see below).

2. Meanwhile for the filling, cook the prunes in their soaking water for 25 minutes or until soft. Drain, then purée in a blender with a little of the cooking liquor, the allspice, vanilla essence and port. Leave to cool and then mix in the chopped walnuts.

3. Place the dough on a floured cloth and pull or roll out (see below). Spread the prune purée over the top of the dough, leaving a small margin at each edge. Fold in the edges and roll up (see below).

4. Brush with melted butter. Place the strudel on a large greased baking sheet. Bake in a preheated oven at Gas Mark 4, 350°F, 180°C for 35 minutes.

5. Mix the honey and concentrated apple juice together. While the strudel is still warm, brush with the honey glaze. Serve warm.

Illustrated on page 62

MAKING A STRUDEL

A strudel is a traditional Austrian or German dish made from paper-thin dough covered with a fruit or cream cheese filling and rolled up like a Swiss roll. The initial kneading is crucial. It will take about 10 minutes by hand or $1\frac{1}{2}$–2 minutes in a food processor, until the dough is elastic and pliable.

1. Mix ingredients, knead, brush with oil, cover and leave for 30 minutes.

2. Pull or roll out the dough to a thin rectangle. Cover with filling.

3. Fold the edges over, roll up from the long side. Seal with water.

RICOTTA CHEESE ～ APRICOT STRUDEL

INGREDIENTS

DOUGH
4oz (125g) wholemeal flour
1 egg yolk
1 tbsp (15ml) sunflower oil
6 tbsp (90ml) warm water

FILLING
8oz (250g) ricotta cheese
¼ tsp almond essence
1lb (500g) fresh apricots, halved
and stoned
2oz (50g) raisins
2oz (50g) blanched almonds,
finely chopped
½oz (15g) butter, melted

GLAZE
2 tsp (10ml) clear honey
2 tsp (10ml) concentrated apple juice

•

NUTRITION PROFILE
*This high-protein pudding is also rich in
Vitamins A, B₁, B₂, C, D and E,
magnesium, iron, zinc and calcium.*

• Per portion •
Carbohydrate: 27.3g
Protein: 7.9g   **Fibre:** 4.3g
Fat: 16.1g   **Calories:** 290

*Ricotta cheese is a very low-fat cheese made from whey not pressed
curds. It has a mild, slightly sweet flavour. When combined with fruit
and nuts it makes a delicious strudel filling and supplies a good
combination of nutrients. Try not to overfill the strudel case, or the
filling may burst out. Serve topped with natural yogurt or smetana.*

Preparation time: 1 hour   Cooking time: 25 mins
Serves 6

METHOD

1. For the dough, place the flour, egg yolk, oil and warm water in a bowl and mix together to form a soft dough. This will take 1½–2 minutes in a blender or food processor. Alternatively, knead vigorously by hand for about 10 minutes, continuously slapping the dough down on the work surface until it is completely pliable.

2. Brush the dough with a little oil, then cover with a warm dish and leave to rest for 30 minutes.

3. Meanwhile, for the filling, mix the ricotta cheese and almond essence together.

4. Place the apricots in a saucepan with a little warm water (or fruit juice) and lightly poach until the juices run.

5. Drain the apricots, then chop and mix with the raisins.

6. Place the strudel dough on a floured cloth and pull it or roll it out gradually to form a large rectangle (see p. 61).

7. Spread on the ricotta cheese, leaving a small margin at each edge. Top with the apricot mixture and almonds.

8. Fold in the edges and even up the rectangle. Then roll up the strudel from the long side. Seal the last edge with a little water (see p. 61).

9. Brush with melted butter.

10. Place the strudel on a baking sheet covered with greaseproof paper. Bake in a preheated oven at Gas Mark 4, 350°F, 180°C for 25 minutes.

11. Mix the honey and concentrated apple juice together. While the strudel is still warm, brush with the honey glaze. Serve warm.

Illustrated opposite

From top: **Ricotta cheese and apricot strudel** (*see above*); **Prune strudel** (*see p. 61*).

PEACH ⁓ NUTMEG CUSHIONS

INGREDIENTS

PANCAKES
1 egg
½ pint (300ml) skimmed milk
4oz (125g) wholemeal flour
pinch salt
¼ tsp grated nutmeg

FILLING
4 peaches, skinned, stoned
and chopped
2 tbsp (30ml) sherry

TOPPING
¼ pint (150ml) smetana
¼ tsp grated nutmeg
1 tsp (5ml) soft brown sugar

•

NUTRITION PROFILE

Rich in iron, calcium, Vitamins A and C, this dessert also contains a small amount of Vitamins B_1, B_{12} and D.

• Per portion •
Carbohydrate: 41.9g
Protein: 8g **Fibre:** 2.8g
Fat: 8.3g **Calories:** 275

This delicious layered pancake pudding is made with an unsweetened peach filling and low-fat smetana topping, yet it tastes extremely rich. Smetana tastes like a cross between yogurt and single cream. It is made from skimmed milk and cream, but has only half the calories of cream.

Preparation time: 60 mins   Cooking time: 15 mins
Serves 4

METHOD

1. For the pancakes, beat the egg and milk together in a blender or food processor. Add the flour, salt and nutmeg and blend again until smooth.

2. Wipe out a frying pan with a little oil. Heat the pan and cook an eighth of the batter (2–3 tbsp/30–45ml), for 2–3 minutes each side. Keep warm while making the remaining 7 pancakes.

3. For the filling, place the peaches in a medium-sized saucepan with the sherry and poach gently for 4–5 minutes, adding a little water if necessary. Spoon some filling into each pancake and fold up to form a small parcel.

4. Layer 4 pancakes on the base of an ovenproof dish. Spread over half the smetana. Then make a second layer with the remaining pancakes and cover with the remaining smetana. Sprinkle on the nutmeg and sugar.

5. Bake in a preheated oven at Gas Mark 4, 350°F, 180°C for 15 minutes.

Illustrated opposite

MAKING PANCAKE CUSHIONS

Pancakes are an immensely versatile way of cooking batter. They can be served with a sweet or savoury accompaniment like a vegetable or fruit purée and rolled, folded or layered. They can be easily adapted by using different types of flour, milk, fat and by adding spices or purées.

1. Fry each pancake in a non-stick pan for 2–3 minutes on each side.

2. Spoon on some filling, then fold over the sides and edges to make a cushion.

3. Using a greased, ovenproof dish, make two layers of filled pancakes.

From top: **Peach and nutmeg cushions** (*see above*); **Cheese pancakes with apple sauce**(*see p. 66*).

SAUCER PANCAKES

INGREDIENTS

PANCAKES
2oz (50g) dried dates, chopped
2oz (50g) margarine
2 eggs, separated
2oz (50g) wholemeal flour

SAUCE
½oz (15g) margarine
4 Conference pears, peeled, cored and
finely chopped
juice of 1 orange
juice of ½ lemon
1 tsp (5ml) grated orange rind
1 tbsp (15ml) Cointreau (optional)

•

NUTRITION PROFILE

*These pancakes are a good source of
Vitamins A, B₁₂, C, D and E.*

• Per portion •
Carbohydrate: 30.2g
Protein: 5.3g **Fibre:** 4.6g
Fat: 15.2g **Calories:** 275

*This old-fashioned recipe makes thick, spongy pancakes, served warm
with a delicious, low-fat pear and orange sauce.*

Preparation time: 20 mins Cooking time: 30 mins
Serves 4

METHOD

1. For the pancakes, place the dates in a saucepan. Cook gently in
a little water for 5–10 minutes, until it makes a thick purée.

2. Beat the margarine, date purée, egg yolks and flour together. In
a separate bowl, whisk the egg whites until soft, then fold in.

3. Wipe out a non-stick frying pan with a little oil. Heat the pan
and pour in a quarter of the batter. Cook on both sides for about 3
minutes. Make 4 thick, saucer-sized pancakes.

4. For the sauce, melt the margarine in a saucepan and gently
cook the pears for 2–3 minutes. Add the fruit juices, rind and
Cointreau, cover and simmer until soft. Beat to a purée. Spoon
some purée on to each pancake, fold in half and serve.

Illustrated opposite

CHEESE PANCAKES WITH APPLE SAUCE

INGREDIENTS

PANCAKES
2 eggs
7oz (200g) skimmed milk soft cheese
(quark)
1 tbsp (15ml) sunflower oil
2oz (50g) wholemeal flour

SAUCE
3 dessert apples, cored
½ tsp ground cloves
juice of ½ lemon
1 tbsp (15ml) brandy

•

NUTRITION PROFILE

*These pancakes are high in protein and are
a good source of Vitamins B₁₂, D and E.*

• Per portion •
Carbohydrate: 19.2g
Protein: 11.8g **Fibre:** 2.7g
Fat: 6.9g **Calories:** 185

*The skimmed milk soft cheese in the batter of these small pancakes
makes this a nutritious, satisfying pudding – ideal after a light salad.*

Preparation time: 15 mins Cooking time: 30 mins
Serves 4

METHOD

1. For the pancakes, beat the eggs, add the soft cheese and oil and
mix thoroughly, then beat in the flour and a pinch of salt.

2. Wipe out a non-stick frying pan with a little oil. Heat the pan
and cook the pancakes, using 1 tbsp (15ml) batter each.

3. For the sauce, place the apples, cloves, lemon juice, brandy
and 1–2 tbsp (15–30ml) water in a saucepan. Cover and simmer
for 10 minutes until the apples are reduced to a sauce.

4. Serve the pancakes flat with the apple sauce over the top.

Illustrated on page 65

From top: **Saucer pancakes** (*see above*); **Cherry oaten pancakes** (*see p. 68*).

CHERRY OATEN PANCAKES

INGREDIENTS

1 egg
¼ pint (150ml) skimmed milk
¼ pint (150ml) natural yogurt
1½oz (40g) rolled oat flakes
1½oz (40g) wholemeal flour
1 tbsp (15ml) wheatgerm
pinch salt

FILLING
1lb (500g) black cherries, stoned
juice of 1 large orange
1 tsp (5ml) arrowroot

•

NUTRITION PROFILE

A good source of protein, calcium, iron and Vitamin C, this recipe also contains Vitamins B$_1$, B$_{12}$ and D.

• Per portion •
Carbohydrate: 36.8g
Protein: 9.7g **Fibre:** 4.8g
Fat: 3.3g **Calories:** 205

These pancakes have the texture of drop scones. Although made with skimmed milk, they taste creamy because of the smooth texture of the oats. Serve with smetana or natural yogurt.

Preparation time: 15 mins Cooking time: 55 mins
Makes 8–10 pancakes

METHOD

1. Mix the egg, milk and yogurt together in a blender for 30 seconds.

2. Add the oats, flour, wheatgerm and salt. Blend again until smooth. Add enough milk to make a pouring consistency.

3. Wipe out a non-stick frying pan with a little oil. Heat the pan and pour in about an eighth of the batter (2–3 tbsp/30–45ml). Cook on both sides for 2–3 minutes. Keep warm, covered with a clean tea-towel, while cooking the remainder.

4. For the filling, purée 12oz (375g) cherries with half of the orange juice in a blender or food processor until smooth.

5. Dissolve the arrowroot in a little water and add to the cherry purée. Bring the mixture to the boil and cook until thickened, stirring. Spoon some cherry filling on to each pancake and fold into four. Arrange in a serving dish.

6. Poach the remaining cherries in the orange juice for 5 minutes. Spoon over the pancakes and serve.

Illustrated on page 67

MOUSSES, SOUFFLES ~AND~ SORBETS

A whipped and chilled dessert is light and clean-tasting after any main course. In these recipes, smetana makes a healthy substitute for cream and fruit adds valuable fibre. A sorbet makes a delicious low-fat alternative to ice cream at any time.

MADEIRA ~AND~ ORANGE SYLLABUB

INGREDIENTS

2 oranges, peeled, segmented
and chopped
3–4 tbsp (45–60ml) Madeira
3–4 fl oz (75–125ml) smetana
3oz (75g) curd cheese
1 tsp (5ml) grated orange rind
2 tbsp (30 ml) orange juice
2 egg whites

•

NUTRITION PROFILE

*This low-calorie syllabub is rich in
Vitamin C.*

• Per portion •
Carbohydrate: 9.6g
Protein: 5.9g   **Fibre:** 1g
Fat: 4.9g   **Calories:** 115

The low-fat combination of smetana and curd cheese, helped by a little alcohol, makes a deliciously rich-tasting syllabub. Use grape juice for a non-alcoholic alternative. If you have enough, reserve some of the orange rind to use as a garnish.

Preparation time: 15 mins (plus chilling time)
Serves 4

METHOD

1. Place the chopped oranges in a bowl. Sprinkle with 1 tbsp (15ml) Madeira and chill.

2. Whisk together the smetana, curd cheese, remaining Madeira, orange rind and juice until quite smooth.

3. Whisk the egg whites until stiff. Fold into the syllabub mixture and chill.

4. Before serving, spoon a portion of orange into each dish and cover with syllabub.

Illustrated on page 71

MAKING A MOUSSE

Mousses are light and fluffy, usually served chilled, and can be savoury or sweet. The traditional French mousses use butter and cream but healthier versions are just as delicious, sweetened with fruit purées, lightened with egg white and set with agar-agar (a vegetable-derived gelling agent). They make an excellent starter or dessert. Fools are more liquid, since they contain no setting agent.

1. Dissolve the agar-agar in a little water.

2. Add to the fruit purée and boil slowly. Simmer for 3 minutes.

3. Cool the purée, then fold in the yogurt and chill.

APRICOT AND CASHEW FOOL

INGREDIENTS

1lb (500g) fresh apricots, halved and stoned
2 tsp (10ml) agar-agar flakes
½ pint (300ml) natural yogurt
1–2oz (25–50g) cashew nut pieces
2 tsp (10ml) clear honey
½ tsp vanilla essence

•

NUTRITION PROFILE

This creamy dessert is rich in Vitamins A and C, and is high in magnesium.

• Per portion •
Carbohydrate: 19.8g
Protein: 6.1g **Fibre:** 4.1g
Fat: 14.3g **Calories:** 220

Nut creams make a delicious, healthy alternative to cream or custard as a base for fools or creamy desserts. Nuts are rich in protein and their fat content, although not low, is unsaturated. You can leave out the nuts if you want a low-fat dessert.

Preparation time: 15 mins (plus chilling time)
Cooking time: about 10 mins
Serves 4

METHOD

1. Reserve 4 apricots, then place the rest in a pan. Simmer in a little water until soft. Purée until smooth.

2. Dissolve the agar-agar flakes in a little water and add to the apricot purée. Bring to the boil, stirring constantly. Simmer for 3 minutes, then leave to cool slightly before folding in the yogurt.

3. Grind the cashew nuts finely in a food processor or grinder. Add enough water to make a thick cream. Sweeten with honey and flavour with vanilla essence. Add the apricot purée and blend until quite smooth. Spoon into 4 individual glasses, decorate with the reserved apricots and serve chilled.

Illustrated opposite

From top: **Madeira and orange syllabub** (*see p. 69*); **Apricot and cashew fool** (*see above*).

BILBERRY MOUSSE

INGREDIENTS

12oz (375g) bilberries
2 tsp (10ml) concentrated apple juice
2 tsp (10ml) agar-agar flakes
4 cloves
6–8 tbsp (90–120ml) smetana
1 egg white
•

NUTRITION PROFILE

This low-calorie dessert is rich in Vitamin C.

• Per portion •
Carbohydrate: 16.7g
Protein: 4g **Fibre:** 3.7g
Fat: 2.8g **Calories:** 105

This delicious, light mousse can be made equally well with blackcurrants, blackberries or tayberries, if bilberries prove difficult to find. Concentrated apple juice helps to sweeten the slightly tart fruit without adding refined sugar to the recipe. A little natural yogurt or smetana on top gives the finishing touch. Smetana is richer than yogurt and its sour cream flavour brings out the delicate flavour of the fruit. This recipe uses agar-agar flakes but you could use the powder form, although remember to use less as it is more concentrated than the flakes.

Preparation time: 30 mins (plus chilling time)
Serves 4

METHOD

1. Wash the bilberries. Place in a saucepan with the concentrated apple juice and poach for 2–3 minutes until the juices run. Purée well in a blender. Sieve, then return to the pan.

2. Dissolve the agar-agar flakes in a little water and add to the bilberry purée. Bring to the boil with the cloves, then simmer for 3–4 minutes, stirring. Remove the cloves. Leave to cool.

3. When cold, stir in the smetana.

4. Whisk the egg white until stiff and fold in. Pile into individual glasses and chill before serving. Serve with yogurt or smetana.

Illustrated opposite

From top: **Apple and gooseberry fool** (*see p. 74*); **Bilberry mousse** (*see above*).

APPLE AND GOOSEBERRY FOOL

INGREDIENTS

1lb (500g) gooseberries, topped
and tailed
2 cooking apples, about 10oz (300g),
peeled, cored and thinly sliced
½ tsp vanilla essence
1–2 tbsp (15–30ml) clear honey
(or to taste)
8oz (250g) curd cheese
7 fl oz (200ml) natural yogurt

•

NUTRITION PROFILE

*This Vitamin C-rich dessert is also a good
source of calcium.*

• Per portion •
Carbohydrate: 13.5g
Protein: 4.5g **Fibre:** 2.6g
Fat: 4.9g **Calories:** 115

*Yogurt and curd cheese combine to make a creamy base for a fruit fool.
For the best texture, leave in the gooseberry pips and skin – this will also
add to the overall fibre content.*

Preparation time: 20 mins (plus chilling time)   Cooking time: 10 mins
Serves 6

METHOD

1. Place the gooseberries and apple slices in a small saucepan,
reserving a few slivers of apple for the garnish. Add the vanilla, a
little honey and 1 tbsp (15ml) water.

2. Cover and cook very gently for about 10 minutes or until the
mixture has reduced to a pulp.

3. Allow to cool slightly, then beat in the curd cheese
and yogurt.

4. Taste for sweetness and add additional honey if necessary.
Serve chilled with the slivers of apple on top.

Illustrated on page 73

BANANA AND MANGO FOOL

INGREDIENTS

1 large mango
5oz (150g) silken tofu
1 banana, peeled

•

NUTRITION PROFILE

*This low-calorie, low-fat dish is a good
source of Vitamins A and C, calcium
and copper.*

• Per portion •
Carbohydrate: 17.2g
Protein: 2.4g **Fibre:** 1.9g
Fat: 1.1g **Calories:** 80

*Tofu makes a useful low-fat, yogurt-like base. To be sure the dish does
not discolour, prepare it about half an hour before serving. Choose a
ripe mango with golden skin; if it is still a little green, leave to ripen in a
warm room.*

Preparation time: 10 mins (plus chilling time)
Serves 4

METHOD

1. Peel the mango and cut the flesh away from the stone,
reserving a few slices for the garnish.

2. In a blender or food processor, mix the tofu, mango and
banana together until smooth.

3. Spoon into 4 dessert dishes and garnish with the slices of
mango. Chill before serving.

Illustrated on page 76

PASSION FRUIT PRALINE

INGREDIENTS

PRALINE
1oz (25g) hazelnuts
1oz (25g) dark brown sugar

BASE
8 passion fruit
1 tbsp (15ml) orange juice
10oz (300g) silken tofu
4oz (125g) curd cheese

•

NUTRITION PROFILE

This dessert is rich in Vitamin C, copper and calcium.

• Per portion •
Carbohydrate: 11.8g
Protein: 8.1g   **Fibre:** 5.2g
Fat: 9.6g   **Calories:** 160

This low-fat tofu and curd cheese mixture, flavoured with passion fruit, transforms into an "egg custard" when baked and blends deliciously with the caramelized hazelnuts (praline). The subtle colouring and flavour of the passion fruit is mouthwatering, but this dish will work equally well with 4 mangoes or 6 peaches.

Preparation time: 30 mins   Cooking time: 20 mins
Serves 4

METHOD

1. For the praline, toast the hazelnuts under a preheated grill for 2–3 minutes. Then rub the skins off with a clean cloth.

2. In a pan, mix the nuts, sugar and 1 tbsp (15ml) water together and heat gently until the sugar dissolves.

3. Raise the heat and boil the mixture for 5–10 minutes or until the nuts pop.

4. Pour the mixture on to a greased baking sheet and allow to cool. When cold, crush in a food processor or grinder, or place between two sheets of greaseproof paper and roll over firmly with a rolling pin.

5. Scoop out the flesh and seeds from the passion fruit and place in a saucepan with the orange juice.

6. Simmer for 2–3 minutes. Strain, sieving out as many seeds as possible.

7. In a blender, or food processor, mix the passion fruit flesh with the tofu and curd cheese.

8. Divide the mixture between 4 ramekin dishes. Top each with a little praline mixture.

9. Bake in a preheated oven at Gas Mark 4, 350°F, 180°C for 15–20 minutes or until just set. Serve warm.

Illustrated on page 76

YULETIDE SOUFFLÉ

INGREDIENTS

4oz (125g) pitted prunes
4oz (125g) raisins
¼ pint (150ml) water
juice of ½ orange
1 tbsp (15ml) brandy
¼ tsp vanilla essence
1 tbsp (15ml) ground almonds
1 tbsp (15ml) wholemeal flour
3 eggs, separated

•

NUTRITION PROFILE

*This high-fibre soufflé is also a rich source
of Vitamins A, B$_{12}$ and D, and is
high in iron.*

• Per portion •
Carbohydrate: 34.8g
Protein: 6.3g   **Fibre:** 7.5g
Fat: 5.1g   **Calories:** 210

*Christmas is traditionally the time not only of good cheer and
hospitality, but also of stodgy food, plenty of alcohol, and endless
sweets, chocolates and mince pies. Not surprisingly, many people find
they simply cannot manage that rich, heavy wedge of Christmas
pudding. This gorgeous light dessert makes a good alternative. It does
not use sugar and is low in fat. Dried fruits and orange juice contribute
vitamins and minerals and lend a sweet, rich taste to the dish.*

Preparation time: 40 mins (plus overnight soaking time)
Cooking time: 25–30 mins
Serves 4

METHOD

1. Soak the prunes and raisins overnight in the water and
orange juice.

2. Gently simmer the prune and raisin mixture for 10 minutes
or until soft.

3. In a blender or food processor, purée the fruits, using a little of
the cooking liquid to form a soft paste.

4. Blend in the brandy, vanilla essence, almonds, flour
and egg yolks.

5. Whisk the egg whites until stiff then fold into the
blended mixture.

6. Wrap a length of greaseproof paper around the top of a small
soufflé dish, so that about 1 inch (2.5cm) overlaps the rim, and
secure with string or tape.

7. Spoon the mixture into the bowl. Bake in a preheated oven at
Gas Mark 5, 375°F, 190°C for 25–30 minutes until well risen and
fairly firm. Remove the paper collar and serve immediately.

Illustrated opposite

Clockwise from top: **Banana and mango fool** (*see p. 74*); **Passion fruit praline** (*see p. 75*); **Yuletide soufflé** (*see above*).

LEMON $\sim$ BANANA ROULADE

INGREDIENTS

BASE
3 eggs, separated
1 tbsp (15ml) clear honey
rind and juice of 1 lemon
2 bananas, peeled and chopped

FILLING
12oz (375g) raspberries

•

NUTRITION PROFILE

*Low in fat and a good source of Vitamins
A, B$_{12}$, C and D, this dessert is also high
in iron and calcium.*

• Per portion •
Carbohydrate: 13.8g
Protein: 5.3g **Fibre:** 5.5g
Fat: 3.1g **Calories:** 100

*This sweet yet sharp-flavoured roulade makes an ideal summer dessert.
It is easy to make and yet never fails to impress. The low-calorie base,
made with lemon and puréed banana, contrasts well with the raspberry
filling and sauce. If you find the mixture will not bind, add a little
wholemeal flour and if raspberries are in short supply, use blackberries,
blackcurrants or strawberries instead.*

Preparation time: 40 mins   Cooking time: 20 mins
Serves 6

METHOD

1. Beat the egg yolks and honey together in a bowl. Add the
lemon rind and half of the lemon juice.

2. Place the bowl over a pan of steaming water and whisk for 5
minutes until the mixture is very stiff. Remove the pan from the
heat and take the bowl off the pan.

3. In a blender or food processor, purée the bananas and
remaining lemon juice. Then fold into the egg yolks.

4. In a separate bowl, whisk the egg whites until stiff. Fold into
the mixture.

5. Line a Swiss roll tin with greaseproof paper. Spread the roulade
mixture evenly over the tin using a palette knife. Bake in a
preheated oven at Gas Mark 5, 375°F, 190°C for 15–20 minutes
or until lightly browned and firm. Turn out on to a clean cloth
covered with greaseproof paper. Carefully peel off the old sheet of
greaseproof paper. Cover with a damp cloth and cool.

6. Mash 8oz (250g) raspberries and spread evenly over the
roulade. Using the fresh sheet of greaseproof paper to lift and
support the roulade, roll it up into a long Swiss roll shape.

7. In a blender, purée the remaining raspberries, sieve and pour a
little sauce over the top just before serving.

Illustrated opposite

Lemon and banana roulade (*see above*).

MANGO ^{AND} PINEAPPLE PARFAIT

INGREDIENTS

7oz (200ml) natural set yogurt
1–2 tsp (5–10ml) clear honey
8oz (250g) mango flesh
8oz (250g) fresh pineapple
flesh, chopped
8oz (250g) strawberries,
hulled (optional)

•

NUTRITION PROFILE

This low-calorie, low-fat dessert is a good source of calcium and Vitamins A and C.

• Per portion •
Carbohydrate: 26.5g
Protein: 3.5g **Fibre:** 2.1g
Fat: 0.5g **Calories:** 120

Yogurt ice cream is delicious, healthy and easy to make. Try to make it on the day it is to be eaten, however, or it may become hard and icy. If you prefer a sweeter taste, you may need to use extra honey.

Preparation time: 15 mins (plus 2–3 hours freezing time)
Serves 4

METHOD

1. Mix together the yogurt and honey. Place in a shallow freezerproof container and freeze until just firm.

2. Transfer to a blender or food processor and mix well.

3. Mix the chopped mango and pineapple together. Add to the yogurt and blend.

4. Return the mixture to the container and freeze for 2 hours or until firm. Scoop out and serve alone or with strawberries.

Illustrated opposite

GRAPEFRUIT ^{AND} PEPPERMINT ICE CREAM

INGREDIENTS

3 grapefruit
1/4 tsp peppermint essence
10oz (300g) silken tofu
2–3 tbsp (30–45ml) soft brown sugar

GARNISH
extra segments of grapefruit

•

NUTRITION PROFILE

This creamy dessert is rich in Vitamin C, calcium and copper.

• Per portion •
Carbohydrate: 29.2g
Protein: 5g **Fibre:** 1.5g
Fat: 2g **Calories:** 150

The unusual combination of peppermint and grapefruit makes a deliciously refreshing ice cream. To prevent the mixture becoming too icy, blend twice and transfer from the freezer to the fridge before serving. This will also enhance the flavour.

Preparation time: 15 mins (plus 2 hours freezing time)
Serves 4

METHOD

1. Halve the grapefruit, scoop out the flesh and dice. Reserve the shells for serving.

2. In a blender or food processor, mix the grapefruit, peppermint essence, tofu and brown sugar together until quite smooth.

3. Pour the mixture into a shallow freezerproof container. Freeze until just firm, then blend until smooth.

4. Pile into the grapefruit halves. Refreeze for a short while only. Garnish with extra segments of grapefruit, allow to defrost a little and serve cold but soft.

Illustrated opposite

From top: **Grapefruit and peppermint ice cream** (*see above*); **Mango and pineapple parfait** (*see above*).

WATERMELON SORBET

INGREDIENTS

8oz (250g) watermelon flesh
2 tbsp (30ml) sweet white wine
or Cointreau
juice of ½ orange
1 tsp (5ml) grated orange rind
1–2 tbsp (15–30ml) clear honey
1–2 egg whites

•

NUTRITION PROFILE

*A good source of Vitamin C, this dessert is
also fat-free and low in calories.*

• Per portion •
Carbohydrate: 10.9g
Protein: 1.6g **Fibre:** 0.4g
Fat: – – **Calories:** 60

*This delicately flavoured sorbet is wonderfully refreshing and is best
eaten on the day it is made. You may find it more economical to buy a
large wedge of watermelon than the entire fruit.*

Preparation time: 20 mins (plus 4–5 hours freezing time)
Serves 4

METHOD

1. Remove the seeds from the watermelon.

2. In a blender or food processor, purée the watermelon with the
wine, orange juice and rind, and the honey.

3. Turn the watermelon mixture into a shallow freezerproof
container. Freeze for 3–4 hours.

4. Purée in a blender until smooth.

5. Whisk the egg white until firm but not dry. Fold into the
watermelon mixture. Refreeze until just firm.

Illustrated opposite

GREEN GRAPE SORBET

INGREDIENTS

1lb (500g) seedless green grapes
2 tbsp (30ml) clear honey
2 tbsp (30ml) concentrated apple juice
1 egg white

•

NUTRITION PROFILE

*This fat-free, low-calorie dessert is a good
source of Vitamin C.*

• Per portion •
Carbohydrate: 30.2g
Protein: 2g **Fibre:** 1.1g
Fat: – – **Calories:** 125

*Frozen sorbets do need a little sweetening to have flavour. In this
recipe, the grapes are naturally very sweet and the honey and
concentrated apple juice contribute added sweetness.*

Preparation time: 15 mins (plus 4–5 hours freezing time)
Serves 4

METHOD

1. Purée the grapes in a blender, then sieve for a smooth liquid.

2. Whisk in the honey and concentrated apple juice.

3. Turn the grape mixture into a shallow freezerproof container.
Freeze for 3–4 hours.

4. Purée in a blender until smooth.

5. Whisk the egg white until firm. Fold into the grape mixture.
Refreeze until just firm.

Illustrated opposite

From top: **Watermelon sorbet** (*see above*); **Green grape sorbet** (*see above*).

CREAMS
AND
SAUCES

These creams and sauces are nutritious, lower fat alternatives to traditional toppings. They are delicious over fresh or cooked fruit, yogurt ice creams, pancakes or muesli and some also make excellent desserts in their own right.

PINEAPPLE AND CAROB CREAM

INGREDIENTS

4oz (125g) dried, stoned dates, chopped
4 tbsp (60ml) tahini
4 tbsp (60ml) carob powder
1lb (500g) fresh pineapple flesh, cubed
1 tsp (5ml) ground ginger
10oz (300g) silken tofu

•

NUTRITION PROFILE

This high-fibre dessert is also a rich source of protein, calcium, magnesium, zinc, copper, iron, niacin and Vitamin C.

• Per portion •
Carbohydrate: 41.7g
Protein: 10.1g **Fibre:** 19.3g
Fat: 11.8g **Calories:** 310

Tahini – a mineral-rich sesame seed cream – forms a good base for cold desserts. This deliciously smooth mixture gains much of its sweetness from carob, a low-fat, high-protein, alternative to cocoa.

Preparation time: 30 mins (plus chilling time)
Serves 4

METHOD

1. Place the dates in a saucepan and cover with a little water. Cook gently for 10–15 minutes, beating well into a thick purée. Cool.

2. Mix the tahini and carob powder together until smooth. Add 3–4 tbsp (45–60ml) of water until the tahini and carob mixture has the consistency of thick cream.

3. Stir in all the remaining ingredients with the cooked date purée and mix in a blender or food processor until smooth. Transfer to a serving dish or individual glasses.

4. Serve well chilled.

Illustrated on page 86

APPLE ᴬᴺᴰ HAZELNUT CREAM

INGREDIENTS

2oz (50g) rolled oats
2oz (50g) hazelnuts
4 dessert apples, cored
juice of ½ orange
1 tsp (5ml) grated orange rind
7fl oz (200ml) natural yogurt

TOPPING
¼ pint (150ml) natural yogurt
•

NUTRITION PROFILE

*This dessert is a good source of calcium
and Vitamins C and E.*

• Per portion •
Carbohydrate: 27.6g
Protein: 7.2g **Fibre:** 3.7g
Fat: 6.7g **Calories:** 190

*This smooth, rich-tasting dessert is based on the original muesli recipe.
For the best flavour, grate the apple very finely and serve
with extra yogurt.*

Preparation time: 15 mins (plus 2 hours soaking and chilling time)
Serves 4

METHOD

1. Soak the oats in 8fl oz (250ml) cold water for at least 2 hours.

2. Toast the hazelnuts lightly under a preheated grill for 3–4
minutes. Cool, then chop very finely.

3. Finely grate the apples, including the skin. Mix with the
soaked oats and remaining ingredients.

4. Divide into individual glasses, top with yogurt, refrigerate and
serve chilled, garnished with hazelnut slices.

Illustrated on page 86

STRAWBERRIES WITH CAROB SAUCE

INGREDIENTS

1 ¼lb (625g) strawberries, hulled

SAUCE
1oz (25g) margarine
1oz (25g) carob powder
¼ tsp vanilla essence
1 tbsp (15ml) maple syrup
1–2 tbsp (15–30ml) orange juice
•

NUTRITION PROFILE

*This low-calorie dessert is rich in Vitamins
C and D.*

• Per portion •
Carbohydrate: 15.7g
Protein: 1.2g **Fibre:** 3.9g
Fat: 5.1g **Calories:** 110

*Carob is a powder like cocoa, but richer in protein, lower in fat and
naturally sweeter. It is also free from stimulants such as caffeine. In
. this recipe it imparts a delightful chocolate flavour to a sauce that goes
well with strawberries – or fresh pears and oranges.*

Preparation time: 25 mins (plus chilling time)
Cooking time: 5 mins
Serves 4

METHOD

1. Divide the strawberries and place in 4 serving dishes.

2. For the sauce, melt the margarine in a saucepan, then stir in
the carob powder, vanilla essence and maple syrup.

3. Cook very gently for 3–4 minutes. (It is most important to
keep the heat low or the carob will burn and curdle.)

4. Thin the sauce with a little orange juice. Leave to cool slightly,
then pour over the strawberries. Refrigerate
and serve chilled.

Illustrated on page 86

CURD CHEESE AND DAMSON SAUCE

INGREDIENTS

12oz (375g) damsons or plums, stoned
and chopped
4oz (125g) curd cheese
2 tbsp (30ml) brandy (optional)

•

NUTRITION PROFILE

*This sauce contains a small but useful
amount of calcium.*

• Per portion •
Carbohydrate: 8.7g
Protein: 3.7g   Fibre: 3.6g
Fat: 5.3g   Calories: 110

*Made from semi-skimmed milk, curd cheese has a medium-fat content
and is denser than most other soft cheeses. Here it enriches the sauce,
making it smooth and creamy, yet much lighter than a roux-based
version. Use the sauce over fruit, ice cream or a pancake base.*

Preparation time: 15 mins
Makes ¾ pint (450ml)

METHOD

1. Place the damsons with 1–2 tbsp (15–30ml) water in a
saucepan. Cook them for 10 minutes or until just soft.

2. Purée in a blender or sieve until smooth.

3. Add the cheese and brandy (if using) and blend again.

4. Warm over a low heat and serve.

Illustrated on page 89

PASSION FRUIT SAUCE

INGREDIENTS

6 passion fruit
3 large oranges
½ tsp arrowroot

•

NUTRITION PROFILE

*This fat-free, low-calorie sauce is high in
fibre and a good source of Vitamin C.*

• Per portion •
Carbohydrate: 10.9g
Protein: 1.6g   Fibre: 6.2g
Fat: – –   Calories: 45

*The glorious colour and flavour of this fruit sauce makes it ideal for
special occasions. Use it on pancakes or yogurt ice creams.*

Preparation time: 20 mins
Makes 7 fl oz (200ml)

METHOD

1. Halve the passion fruit and scoop out the flesh.

2. Halve and squeeze the oranges, then mix the juice with the
passion fruit flesh in a saucepan. Heat the mixture gently
for 3–4 minutes.

3. Sieve the juice to remove the passion fruit seeds.

4. Dissolve the arrowroot in a little water and mix into the fruit
juice. Bring to the boil, cover and simmer for 3 minutes. Serve
hot or cold.

Illustrated on page 89

From top: **Pineapple and carob cream** (*see p.* 84); **Strawberries with carob sauce** (*see p.* 85);
Apple and hazelnut cream (*see p.* 85).

APPLE AND YOGURT SAUCE

INGREDIENTS

3 cooking apples, peeled, cored
and diced
3 tbsp (45ml) concentrated apple juice
3 tbsp (45ml) water
7 fl oz (200ml) natural yogurt
1 tsp (5ml) cornflour

•

NUTRITION PROFILE

*This low-fat sauce is rich in Vitamin C
and calcium.*

• Per portion •
Carbohydrate: 17.1g
Protein: 2.8g   **Fibre:** 2g
Fat: 0.5g   **Calories:** 80

Yogurt plays an invaluable part in healthy eating. It is a natural antibiotic, helps to discourage harmful bacteria, is easily digested and very soothing on an upset or sensitive stomach. An extremely versatile ingredient, you can use it in soups, sauces, dips and sweet or savoury dressings. It adds a sharp flavour and helps to lighten this fruit sauce, which is delicious over muesli, fruit or a biscuit base. Yogurt makes a healthy alternative to cream, and an easy way to eke out cottage cheese or skimmed milk soft cheese (quark). It is, of course, very tasty on its own, with perhaps a little honey. When heating yogurt, add cornflour to prevent it separating.

Preparation time: 20 mins   Cooking time: 10 mins
Makes ½ pint (300ml)

METHOD

1. Place the apples with the apple juice and water in a saucepan. Stew gently until tender. Purée in a blender until smooth.

2. Mix the yogurt with the cornflour. Add to the apple purée.

3. Simmer gently for 5 minutes to heat through and cook the cornflour, stirring constantly. Serve warm.

Illustrated opposite

From top: **Apple and yogurt sauce** (*see above*); **Passion fruit sauce** (*see p. 87*); **Curd cheese and damson sauce** (*see p. 87*).

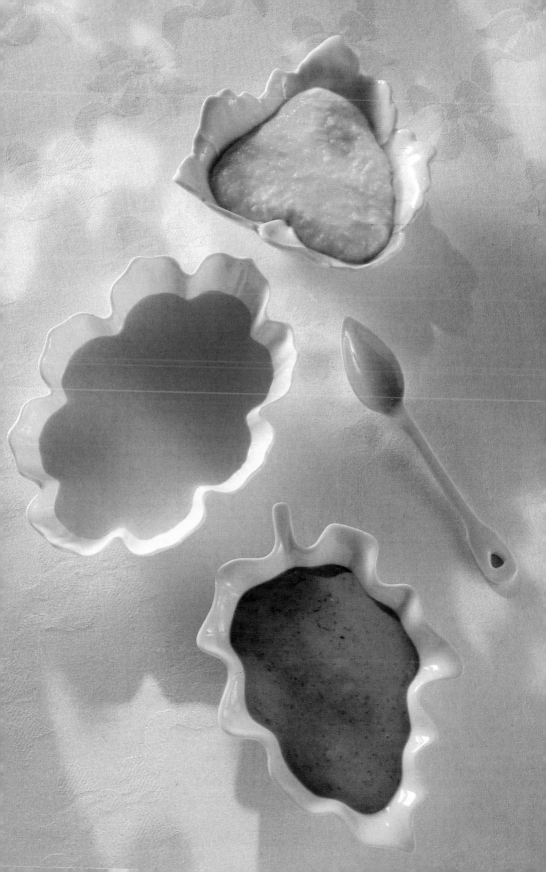

NUTRITION CHARTS

The evidence that diet and disease are linked continues to mount. Eating a well-balanced diet can help to keep you in good health, or even improve your health. Medical conditions prevalent in today's society, including heart disease, diabetes, cancer of the bowel and even minor ailments like migraines can be wholly or partially eradicated by changing the foods we eat. In 1983, The National Advisory Committee on Nutrition Education produced a report on the links between diet and health. The following pages translate the recommendations into a palatable formula for a healthy diet. There is no need to forego our favourite foods in an effort to improve our diet; it is largely a question of re-thinking the quality and the type of food we eat and getting the balance right.

USING THE NUTRITION PROFILES

Our diet is made up of three major nutrients: proteins, fats and carbohydrates (including fibre, starch and sugar), each of which contributes to our calorie intake. But how much of each should we eat every day and which foods contain them? The charts (below) give our recommended daily intakes and list the foods richest in each nutrient. This information will in turn help you to use the nutrition profiles given with each recipe, to plan a balanced day's eating. A recipe that contains 15g of fibre, provides half your daily requirement of 30g per day.

CARBOHYDRATE

Carbohydrates, which are made up of sugars, starch and fibre, are the major source of energy in the diet. Excess is stored as fat. Unrefined carbohydrates are more nutritious than refined. Unrefined starches are richer in vitamins, help to maintain a steady blood sugar level and are lower in calories.

ADVICE: Eat more unrefined carbohydrates (wholemeal grains, bread and pasta, fresh fruit and vegetables and pulses).

Rich Sources of Carbohydrate

Recommended daily intake: 250–375g†

Split peas	1oz (25g) dry weight	Contains	71g
Lentils	1oz (25g) dry weight	..	67g
Potato	7oz (200g) baked	..	41g
Banana	1 (6oz/175g)	..	34g
Dried dates	2oz (50g)	..	32g
Wholemeal bread	2 slices (2½oz/70g)	..	29g
Dried prunes	2oz (50g)	..	20g
Black grapes	4oz (125g)	..	19g
Brown rice	2oz (50g) dry weight	..	16g
Beetroot	4oz (125g) cooked	..	12g

FIBRE

High-fibre foods help to keep the digestive system in good working order and in some cases lower cholesterol levels.
ADVICE: Eat more fibre (fresh and dried fruit and vegetables, wholegrains and pulses).

Rich Sources of Fibre

Recommended daily intake: 25–30g†

Dried apricots	2oz (50g)	Contains	12g
Peas	4oz (125g) fresh or frozen	..	11g
Blackcurrants	4oz (125g) stewed, no sugar	..	11g
Figs	2oz (50g) about 3 figs	..	9g
Raspberries	4oz (125g)	..	9g
Haricot beans	4oz (125g) cooked	..	9g
Spinach	4oz (125g) cooked	..	8g
Prunes	2oz (50g) dry weight	..	8g
Almonds	2oz (50g) shelled	..	7g
Butter beans	4oz (125g) cooked	..	6g
Wholemeal bread	2 slices (2½oz/70g)	..	6g
Potato	7oz (200g) baked	..	5g

PROTEIN

Protein is needed for growth and for the maintenance of healthy muscles and tissue. Vegetables and dairy products contain different forms of protein and by eating a wide range of food combinations, such as muesli with milk, pasta with cheese or beans with rice you can obtain complete, high-quality proteins.
ADVICE: Obtain main protein requirements from vegetable-based foods (grains, cereals, pulses).

Rich Sources of Protein

Recommended daily intake: 53–90g (men) 48–68g (women)†

Amounts expressed in typical portions

Soya flour	2oz (50g)	Contains	18g
Cottage cheese	4oz (125g) carton	..	17g
Cheddar cheese	2oz (50g)	..	13g
Peanuts	2oz (50g) shelled	..	12g
Skimmed milk	½ pint (300ml)	..	10g
Cashew nuts	2oz (50g)	..	9g
Egg	1 egg, size 3	..	6g
Wholemeal bread	2 slices (2½oz/70g)	..	6g
Potato	8oz (250g) baked	..	5g

† As recommended in Great Britain by the Department of Health and Social Security

FATS

There are three sources of fat: saturated, monounsaturated and polyunsaturated. Each of the three types are present in fatty foods in varying proportions. Saturated fats increase blood cholesterol levels, which can lead to heart disease. Polyunsaturated fats help to lower cholesterol levels.

ADVICE: Eat less fat. Within your daily allowance, include less saturated and more polyunsaturated fat (vegetable oils, nuts).

Sources of Polyunsaturated Fat

Recommended daily intake: 77–117g (about 35% of daily calories, of which only 15% (33–50g) should be saturated).†

Walnuts	2oz (50g)	*Contains*	26gF	*incl.*	18gPUF
Polyunsaturated margarine	1oz (25g)	..	20gF	..	15gPUF
Brazil nuts	2oz (50g)	..	31gF	..	12gPUF
Soya bean oil	1 tbsp (15ml)	..	12gF	..	7gPUF
Sunflower seed oil	1 tbsp (15ml)	..	12gF	..	6gPUF
Oatmeal	2tbsp (1oz/25g)	..	2gF	..	1gPUF

CALORIES

Almost everything we eat is turned into energy, which is measured in calories (sometimes called kilocalories), and used up by the body in activity and in keeping the body working. Calorie needs depend on sex, age, weight and activity, but if calorie intake constantly outstrips demand, body weight increases.

Calorie values

Recommended daily intake: Men 3,000 cals Women 2,200 cals†

Foods high in calories

Nuts	2oz (50g) almonds	*Contains*	285
	peanuts	..	285
	walnuts	..	265
Cheddar cheese	2oz (50g)	..	230
Avocado pear	½ (3½oz/100g) flesh	..	205
Butter/margarine	¾oz (20g)	..	185
Pastry	1½oz (40g)	..	165

Foods with average calories

Brown rice	2oz (50g) dry weight	..	180
Potato	7oz (200g) baked	..	175
Wholemeal pasta	2oz (50g) dry weight	..	160
Wholemeal bread	2 slices (2½oz/70g)	..	150
Soft curd cheese	2oz (50g)	..	95
Butterbeans	1oz (25g) dry weight	..	70
Mung beans	1oz (25g) dry weight	..	60

Foods low in calories

Cottage cheese	4oz (125g)	..	110
Skimmed milk	½ pint (300ml)	..	100
Yogurt	5oz (150g) natural	..	80
Fresh fruit	1 apple/orange	..	50
Low-fat soft cheese	2oz (50g)	..	40
Vegetables	4oz (125g) leeks	..	30
	4oz (125g) mushrooms	..	15

PLANNING BALANCED MEALS

It is easy to get the right amounts of carbohydrates, protein, fibre, fat, calories and the various vitamins and minerals from a vegetarian diet if you follow a few basic guidelines.

• Try to have three evenly sized meals a day. This keeps the blood sugar level steady and avoids taxing the digestive system and internal organs.

• If you have to eat between meals, have some fresh or dried fruit; crisp, raw vegetables; a piece of toast, sweetened with dried fruit or honey; or some nuts.

• Try to have one grain-based meal a day, such as toast for breakfast and rice or pasta at a main meal.

• Try to have at least one salad-based meal a day.

• Have one meal based on vegetarian protein (cheese, beans, nuts) each day and, if you are not vegetarian, limit animal protein (fish, eggs, meat) to about 3 times a week.

• Finish meals with fresh, stewed or dried fruit in place of high-fat, high-sugar desserts, such as cakes, pastries, ice creams.

• Try to limit tea or coffee to no more than 5 cups a day (or drink herbal tea and cereal coffee). Keep alcohol intake down to 2 glasses of wine or 1 pint of beer or cider a day.

SUGGESTIONS FOR DAILY PORTIONS

In an average day it is easy to eat too much of one sort of food and not enough of another. The chart (below) suggests how many portions of each type of food you should aim to eat with limited examples of how to obtain them.

NUMBER OF PORTIONS	FOOD	EXAMPLES
4	Dairy	1 cup skimmed milk • 5oz (150g) natural yogurt • 1oz (25g) cheese • 1 egg
4	Vegetables	4oz (125g) spinach • 4oz (125g) carrots • 4oz (125g) broccoli
3	Fruits	Glass unsweetened orange juice • 1 apple or orange • 2oz (50g) dried prunes
4	Grains	2 slices wholemeal bread • 4oz (125g) brown rice • 2oz (50g) pasta
4	Beans and nuts	2oz (50g) cashew nuts • 2oz (50g) sesame seeds • 4oz (125g) cooked beans

VITAMINS

Alcohol, the contraceptive pill, caffeine, smoking and food processing slows the absorption of some vitamins, so raising daily needs. Vegetarians should check their Vitamin B_{12} intake. (1,000mg = 1g 1,000μg = 1mg).

VITAMIN	USES	DAILY INTAKE†	RICH VEGETARIAN SOURCES
A	Promotes night vision, healthy eyes, skin, hair, nails and internal mucous membranes. Helps the utilization of fat and Vitamin C and the action of the liver and thyroid.	750μg*	4oz (125g) watercress: 3,750μg ● 4oz (125g) carrots: 2,500μg ● 4oz (125g) cooked spinach: 1,250μg ● 2oz (50g) dried apricots: 300μg ● 4oz (125g) broccoli: 521μg ● ½ pint (300ml) whole milk: 116μg ● 1 medium tomato (3oz/75g): 75μg ● 1 egg (2oz/50g): 70μg
B_1 (thiamin)	Helps to metabolize carbohydrate. Keeps the nervous system, brain, muscles, and heart functioning well. Some losses with cooking.	1.2mg	2 slices wholemeal bread (2½oz/70g): 0.2mg ● 2oz (50g) brazil nuts: 0.5mg ● 2oz (50g) peanuts: 0.5mg ● 4oz (125g) cooked peas: 0.3mg ● 3tsp (¼oz/7g) yeast extract: 0.2mg ● 1 tbsp (¼oz/7g) wheatgerm: 0.1mg
B_2 (riboflavin)	Keeps skin, eyes, nails, hair and lips healthy. With thiamin, helps to metabolize carbohydrates. Helps thyroid function.	1.6mg**	½ pint (300ml) skimmed milk: 0.6mg ● 4oz (125g) mushrooms: 0.5mg ● 2oz (50g) almonds: 0.5mg ● 5oz (150ml) natural yogurt: 0.4mg ● 2oz (50g) Cheddar cheese: 0.3mg ● 1 egg (2oz/50g): 0.2mg
Niacin (Vitamin B_3)	Keeps brain and nervous system functioning well. Helps to metabolize food and to synthesize hormones.	18mg**	2oz (50g) peanuts: 8mg ● 3 tsp (¼oz/7g) yeast extract: 4mg ● 4oz (125g) mushrooms: 5mg ● 4oz (125g) cooked broad beans: 4mg ● 2oz (50g) dried peaches: 3mg ● 2 slices wholemeal bread (2½oz/70g): 3mg
B_6	Helps the body to use protein, fats and iron. Important in nerve, brain, blood and muscle functioning. Controls cholesterol levels. Activates enzymes.	No official guideline but 1.5–2mg advised**	1 tbsp (⅛oz/3.5g) bran: 0.04mg ● 1 tbsp (¼oz/7g) wheatgerm: 0.07mg ● 3 tsp (¼oz/7g) yeast extract: 0.09mg ● 2 tbsp (1oz/25g) oatmeal: 0.15mg ● 2oz (50g) walnuts: 0.37mg ● 2oz (50g) soya flour: 0.28mg ● 2oz (50g) hazelnuts: 0.28mg ● 1 banana (5oz/150g): 0.77mg
B_{12}	Helps to form blood cells and metabolize food. Prevents pernicious anaemia. Works with folic acid. Vegetarians, especially vegans, may be deficient.	2μg	1 egg yolk (¾oz/20g): 0.98μg ● 1 egg (2oz/50g): 0.85mg ● 2oz (50g) Cheddar cheese: 0.75μg ● 2oz (50g) Parmesan cheese: 0.75μg ● 2oz (50g) Brie and low-fat soft cheeses: 0.6μg ● 3 tsp (¼oz/7g) yeast extract: 0.04μg ● 4oz (125g) carton cottage cheese: 0.63μg
Folic Acid	Helps form red blood cells, and genetic material, metabolize protein and sugars, and make antibodies. Promotes healthy skin and wards off anaemia.	400μg**	4oz (125g) cooked spinach: 175μg ● 2oz (50g) raw endive: 165μg ● 4oz (125g) cooked broccoli: 138μg ● 4oz (125g) cooked Brussel sprouts: 109μg ● 3 tsp (¼oz/7g) yeast extract: 71μg ● 2oz (50g) peanuts: 55μg ● 2oz (50g) almonds: 48μg ● 1tbsp (¼oz/7g) wheatgerm: 23.1μg
C	Helps to prevent disease and infection, increases anti-bodies and energy levels. Aids calcium and oxygen metabolism, and iron absorption, lowers cholesterol.	30mg	1 red or green pepper (5oz/150g): 130mg ● 4oz (125g) blackcurrants: 250mg ● juice of 1 lemon: 80 mg ● 4oz (125g) strawberries: 75mg ● 4oz (125g) boiled spring cabbage: 31mg ● 4oz (125g) boiled potatoes: 18mg ● 3 sprigs parsley (¼oz/7g): 11mg ● 4oz (125g) spinach: 6mg
D	Helps in absorption of calcium and phosphorus. Keeps heart, nervous system, eyes, bones and teeth healthy.	2.5μg***	¾oz (20g) margarine: 1.6μg ● 1 egg yolk (¾oz/20g): 1.0μg ● 2oz (50g) Cheddar: 0.1μg ● 2oz (50g) Parmesan cheese: 0.1μg ● ½ pint (300ml) whole milk: 0.1μg
E	Protects cell walls. Helps wounds to heal quickly. Relieves heart conditions. Stimulates immune system. Deficiency very rare.	No guideline in UK.	2oz (50g) hazelnuts: 10.5mg ● 2oz (50g) almonds: 10mg ● 1 tbsp (15ml) sunflower oil: 7.2mg ● 2oz (50g) peanuts: 4.05mg ● 2oz (50g) Brazil nuts: 3.25mg ● ¾oz (20g) margarine: 1.6mg ● 1 tbsp (¼oz/7g) wheatgerm: 0.8mg

† As recommended in Great Britain by the Department of Health and Social Security

MINERALS

A diet rich in vegetable-based foods should supply plenty of minerals. Pregnant women and growing children may need a little more, and alcohol, smoking, caffeine and the Pill can also increase daily needs.

MINERAL	USES	DAILY INTAKE†	RICH MINERAL SOURCES
Iron	Essential for the formation of haemoglobin and to carry oxygen. Vegans, vegetarians and children may be deficient.	Men: 10mg Women: 12mg**	1oz (25g) blackstrap molasses: 4mg ● 1 tbsp (¹/₈oz/3.5g) bran: 0.4mg ● 1 tbsp (¹/₄oz/7g) wheatgerm: 0.7mg ● 3 sprigs parsley (¹/₄oz/7g): 0.6mg ● 2oz (50g) soya flour: 3.5mg ● 2oz (50g) dried peaches: 3.4mg
Calcium	Works with Vitamin D to promote healthy bones, teeth and nerves. Deficiency can cause osteoporosis in older people.	500mg**	2oz (50g) Parmesan cheese: 610mg ● 2oz (50g) Cheddar cheese: 400mg ● 4oz (125g) cooked spinach: 750mg ● 2oz (50g) Brie and soft cheeses: 190mg ● 3 sprigs parsley (¹/₄oz/7g): 30mg ● 2oz (50g) dried figs: 140mg
Magnesium	Helps synthesis of protein and fats and use of calcium, potassium, sodium and Vitamin B₆. Maintains healthy heart beat.	No official guideline but 200–400mg advised	2oz (50g) brazil nuts: 205mg ● 2oz (50g) almonds: 130mg ● 2oz (50g) soya flour: 120mg ● 2oz (50g) peanuts: 90mg ● 2oz (50g) wholemeal flour: 70mg ● 2oz (50g) walnuts: 65mg ● 2 slices wholemeal bread (2¹/₂oz/70g): 65mg
Potassium	Acts with sodium to regulate the body fluids, maintain the acid/alkali balance and to transport nerve impulses to muscles. Dietary deficiency rare.	No official guidelines in UK	2oz (50g) dried apricots: 940mg ● 2oz (50g) soya flour: 830mg ● 1oz (25g) blackstrap molasses: 732mg ● 2oz (50g) dried peaches: 550mg ● 2oz (50g) dried figs: 505mg ● 2oz (50g) sultanas: 430mg ● 3 tsp (¹/₄oz/7g) yeast extract: 182mg ● 3 sprigs parsley (¹/₄oz/7g): 97mg
Zinc	Essential for enzyme action. Aids vision and bone growth. Zinc absorption is reduced by a high-fibre diet.	15mg	2oz (50g) brazil nuts: 2.1mg ● 2oz (50g) Parmesan cheese: 2mg ● 2oz (50g) Cheddar cheese: 2mg ● 2oz (50g) almonds: 1.6mg ● 2oz (50g) peanuts or walnuts: 1.5mg ● 2 slices wholemeal bread (2¹/₂oz/70g): 1.4mg

FINDING HEALTHIER ALTERNATIVES

Healthy eating does not have to be a deprivation. By simply replacing high-fat, high-sugar and high-salt foods with more nutritious alternatives, you can dramatically improve your diet. Here are some suggestions.

TYPICAL FOODS	GOOD ALTERNATIVES
jam/marmalade	low-sugar, high-fruit preserves
fruit stewed with sugar	fruit stewed with concentrated juice
fruit canned in syrup	fruit canned in natural juices
sweetened carbonated drinks	sparkling or natural fruit juices, still or sparkling mineral water
sugary snacks	fresh fruit or dried fruit
sugar on cereals	fresh fruit or dried fruit
confectionery	fresh fruit, dried fruit or fruit bars
salted cocktail snacks	unsalted nuts, raw vegetable strips
full-cream milk	fresh skimmed milk, soya milk
cream, evaporated or condensed milk	natural yogurt, smetana, silken tofu, buttermilk or natural fromage frais
full-fat soft cheeses	skimmed milk soft cheese (quark), cottage cheese, ricotta, tofu or brie

TYPICAL FOODS	GOOD ALTERNATIVES
full-fat hard cheeses	Edam or Gouda, or low-fat cheese
meat	pulses, lentils, nuts, grains, pastas, tofu
butter, hard margarine	polyunsaturated margarine
chips	jacket potatoes or boiled in skins
unspecified vegetable oil	oil high in polyunsaturates, e.g. safflower, sunflower, soya
salt	herbs and spices, shoyu, gomashio
cream cakes	wholemeal fruit breads
tea	herb teas
chocolate/cocoa	carob
white bread	wholemeal, rye, flavoured bread
fried vegetables	steamed, baked or raw vegetables
lard	vegetable fat or oil

* Requirement increased in lactating women

* * Requirement increased in pregnant and lactating women

* * * Requirement increased in young children, pregnant and lactating women

INDEX

Page numbers in **bold** refer to the illustrations

ACKNOWLEDGMENTS

EDITOR: Rosanne Hooper
ART EDITOR: Anita Ruddell
ASSISTANT EDITOR: Rebecca Abrams
DESIGNER: Sally Powell
EDITORIAL ASSISTANT:
  Sophie Galleymore-Bird

EDITORIAL DIRECTOR: Alan Buckingham
ART DIRECTOR: Stuart Jackman

PHOTOGRAPHIC ART DIRECTION:
  Patrick McLeavey & Partners
PHOTOGRAPHER: Graham Miller
HOME ECONOMIST: Jane Miller
STYLIST: Pip Kelly
ILLUSTRATOR: Nancy Anderson

TYPESETTING: Tradespools, Frome
REPRODUCTION AND PRINTING:
  Arnoldo Mondadori, Verona, Italy

Author's acknowledgments
Sarah Brown would like to thank Ian Burleigh
and Roselyne Masselin for all their help.

Dorling Kindersley would like to thank: Barbara
Croxford for her help with the recipes; Dr
Michèle Sadler for her work on the Nutrition
profiles; Fred and Cathy Gill, Gill Aspery and
Janice Lacock for invaluable proof-reading;
Hilary Bird for the index; The Vegetarian
Society and The Fresh Fruit and Vegetable
Information Bureau for their help.